THE ASPIE TEEN'S SURVIVAL GUIDE

J. D. Kraus

The Aspie Teen's Survival Guide

All marketing and publishing rights guaranteed to
and reserved by:

FUTURE HORIZONS INC.

721 W. Abram Street
Arlington, Texas 76013
800-489-0727
817-277-0727
817-277-2270 (fax)
E-mail: info@FHautism.com
www.FHautism.com

ISBN: 9781935274162

Publisher's Cataloging-In-Publication Data
(Prepared by The Donohue Group, Inc.)

Kraus, J. D.
  The Aspie teen's survival guide / J.D. Kraus.

  p. ; cm.

  Includes bibliographical references and index.
  ISBN: 978-1-935274-16-2

  1. Asperger's syndrome in adolescence--Handbooks, manuals, etc. 2. Teenagers with social disabilities--Handbooks, manuals, etc. 3. Asperger's syndrome--Patients--Life skills guides. 4. Parents of autistic children--Handbooks, manuals, etc. I. Title.

RJ506.A9 K73 2010
618.92/858/8

Printed in the United States of America.

Dedication

To Jerry Newport and Sean Barron, who encouraged
me to write this book.

To Mr. Dave Cummings, who helped me as my Creative Writing
teacher and as a friend. And lastly, to my parents
for their loving support.

Table of Contents

Foreword

By Rudy Simone

Technically, I never graduated from high school. I barely went, completing, as far as I can remember, 8th grade. I knew I was gifted, as did some of my teachers and staff. They had told my mother, but she didn't pay much attention; in those days, many girls didn't go to college and the phrase "too smart for her own good" was one I often heard aimed in my direction. I had taught myself to read before kindergarten and had a sophisticated way of speaking for my age (hyperlexia) so it was thought I was merely precocious. My intellectual mind was strong—it wasn't until adolescence hit that my idiosyncrasies turned into problems, mostly of a social nature.

I'd always had friends, although I had thought of them more as either props on my stage, supporting actors, or an audience—I'd sing and make up stories to tell them, or force them to be in one of my plays. I saw the need for only one *real* friend at a time, but since it was apparent that even she needed others, I grudgingly went along with it. Once I reached high school, singing, performing, and monologuing no longer worked. Relationships had to be reciprocal, which meant I had little control. Not being able to read people, I was suddenly completely out of my element. Kids I had thought were friends now bullied me daily in the transition from childhood to adolescence, bullying that was often very physical and very violent. I developed mutism first at home, then at school and in my so-called social life. I then developed an ulcer and soon suffered fainting episodes and memory blackouts. My love for information and learning was then overshadowed by my fear of school—the larger building, more auditory lectures in class, but mostly my fear of other kids. I had gone from class clown to class ghost, afraid of everything and everyone.

I skipped class after class until I was so far behind, I even failed English, my most beloved subject. I couldn't believe it—me, the kid who had a college reading level at age ten and won a statewide writing competition at twelve! I quit 9th grade right after we moved towns. The transition of being in a new place, fear of new bullies, as well as the shame of failing was too much. J.D. Kraus also fled school in 9th grade, causing panic for his parents and his school, but afterward, his already supportive network stepped up their game and he got the help he needed. The fact that this book exists means that no other teen with Asperger's has to feel so alone, confused, and ashamed. They can get the help they need, turn and face their fears, and continue their studies for as long as they want or need. Not having a solid education has impacted my self-esteem, my credibility, and my finances in more ways than I care to recount.

In the 1970s and at the start of the '80s, no one knew of Hans Asperger and his work more than three decades earlier. Even if they had, they wouldn't have recognized Asperger's Syndrome in me, because I did not fit the male prototype—we have subtle differences that are still making it difficult for experts to recognize AS in girls, although recently that has taken an encouraging turn. No one would have guessed that the shy girl who was an outgoing, exemplary student in her formative years was affected by a mild form of autism! The teenagers reading this book have something I did not—a diagnosis, even if it is only self-diagnosis. Many people self-diagnose before the official verdict. If it fits and if the information is working for you, use it, but do try and get an official diagnosis, even if just for your own peace of mind. It may be a piece of paper, but just like a diploma or degree, it lets others know what you have so you don't have the added burden of proof. Many adults are afraid of an AS diagnosis on their record and are worried the information may be used against them, but from my experience, many are helped and aided by their employers and tutors once armed with this crucial explanation.

Asperger's is an explanation; it is not an excuse. There's a fine line between the two. Many parents, partners and professionals are concerned that people on the spectrum are becoming obsessed with AS. It is important to research and understand your Asperger's Syndrome thoroughly, read all you can, discuss it until you become very comfortable talking about it, then go back to your life, even while you work through your challenges. Asperger's itself should not become your special interest. It is the motor *behind* your special interests, and the diligence and passion with which you pursue them. While some of us do write books, lecture, and become consultants, by and large AS is not our main occupation. It would be remiss to channel all our energies into that and forget that there are inventions, formulas, books, songs, art, and other things to explore and to create.

You are so lucky to know about Asperger's. I wish I'd had a diagnosis when I was young, although I may have rejected it initially, thinking it meant I was flawed. Well, guess what—we all have flaws. Autistic, neurotypical, everyone has frailties. That too is an important thing to remember as you go through life—some people will be kind to you immediately, seem to understand and accept you more easily than others. Others might not be so kind, but even they might understand you if given a little education about Asperger's and by witnessing your good qualities in action. These are both plentiful and formidable: *focus, honesty, thinking outside the box, diligence* and even a *higher level of fluid intelligence*, which is the ability to make novel connections and understand things you haven't even been taught yet. There are many more besides. Don't hide yourself away from the world because you have a fight-or-flight reaction to others. Stand your ground and turn it around. We all need people at times, and the world most definitely needs us.

I did receive my GED with a perfect score, and did go on to college pre-diagnosis, never successfully completing a higher degree although I have managed many short term qualifications. If I had to do it again,

I would have support, an IEP, and I'd either graduate high school early and enter college early, or else I would try to get into a special school for gifted kids and/or kids with ASDs. Following that, I'd go to college and study in my field of interest, and work with staff to get special accommodations if I needed them. Many of us want to start working in our field right away, and I dropped out of college initially for that reason. It is important to realize that what we can handle intellectually might be much more than what we can handle emotionally and physically. Be patient and see your diploma and degree through so that you can work in your field of interest. Nowadays, it is exceedingly difficult to get anything but the most menial of jobs without a degree. Lower level jobs such as waitressing, stock boy, secretary or cashier, often require the one thing we don't have in abundance—people skills! Be realistic—dream your life but then research the best and most tangible way to make that happen. Have a few different paths mapped out that you can travel to give you career satisfaction and financial stability. Money is the key to living in the type of environment you need—e.g., a quiet, private house as opposed to a shoddy apartment building with lots of noise and strangers.

But I am getting ahead of this book. *The Aspie Teen's Survival Guide* will take you through all the steps to get you through high school and you can keep on using these tips the rest of your life. J. D. Kraus provides invaluable advice on every aspect of teen life with AS—from friendships and socializing to homework and driving to meltdowns and medications. This book is chock full of great information, whether he's talking about transitioning, seating arrangements, the color of test paper, or feeling bad about not being able to catch the ball in gym class. (Did you think you were the only one?) He gives sage and sound advice to teens, parents, teachers, and other professionals, to help smooth the whole process for everyone. At the same time, he cautions that no two individuals are alike and you can play around with his recipe to find what works for you. This book will also be a good read for adults who are newly diagnosed and want some simple re-framing in looking back at their own scholastic life, which might bear some scars that need healing.

The Aspie Teen's Survival Guide is so personal, so engaging, and so immediate, it's like having a big brother or mentor who's "been there" show you the way to minimize your scrapes and bumps. No matter what your connection to Asperger's or where you are in your AS journey, this is an invaluable source of validation, inspiration, and information.

Rudy Simone
Author of *Asperger's on the Job* and *Aspergirls*

Chapter 1

What Is Asperger's Syndrome?

What do you think when you hear the word *syndrome*? Is it a disease? A disorder? According to scientists, Asperger's Syndrome (AS) is a Pervasive Developmental Disorder (PDD) that is arguably related to autism.[1] Asperger's Syndrome is a disorder in which normal-looking people are superb at certain things, but humorously incapable of others. However, there are hills and dips within it, sort of like a roller coaster.

People with this disability are challenged by social interactions, particularly with the nonverbal aspects of communication, including understanding facial expressions and body language.[2] Seldom do people with AS form lasting relationships, especially close ones. As an individual with Asperger's Syndrome, I have formed only one or two really close relationships outside of my family.

I have written this book in first person. It will come in most handy for teenagers with Asperger's, but will also be helpful for the friends and families of this unusual person.

MYSELF

I always wondered why I was so different from everyone else. Why did I have only a few friends? Why couldn't I just be normal? I couldn't keep wondering all my life why I was so different, so I sought answers.

In 2003, I began therapy. I asked my therapist the kinds of questions I had been asking myself. He gave me a book to read about a disorder called Asperger's Syndrome (AS). It was written by a youth around my age who has this disorder. I read the book in two weeks. Not only were many of my questions answered, but I also didn't feel so alone. Around this time I read somewhere that there are an estimated six million cases of people with AS worldwide, and millions more who have similar disorders.

I came to realize that this "disability" was not a putrid disease or a curse. At that point, I stopped worrying about being different. In fact, I learned that being different is really swell. After I read this book, I looked up as much information as I could about Asperger's Syndrome, and I even attended a convention about it.

My mother, bless her heart, has probably taken a more "in-depth" look at AS. She has always told me I was special and her "little man." The first sign of my uniqueness was revealed when I was five. I don't remember the details well, but I had to take a developmental test in kindergarten. One part of the test was to name as many animals as I could in a minute.

The tester had a stopwatch and said, "Okay. Ready? One, two, three, go."

When she said, "Go," I ran out the door. I left a few oblivious adults behind. Since then, my devoted parents have wondered what drives this "little man."

THE THING ABOUT AS

At a convention I went to with my mother, I met a cool guy named Jerry Newport. He's a spokesperson for an organization that supports people with AS. Listening to the story of his struggle with why he was different from everyone else made me feel sympathetic, and helped me understand why I was so different.

One of the books he has written, *Your Life is Not A Label*, which is another compelling book I read on Asperger's Syndrome, says that people are not limited in any fashion, whether they have a "syndrome" or not.[3]

Mr. Newport told me that, years ago, a college friend of his asked him, "If you don't act like you care about yourself, then why should anyone else care?"

If you can't accept having AS, or don't have feelings for yourself, then who else should care? As I said before, Asperger's Syndrome is not a disease or a curse. It means you have an extra challenge to accept and live with. It doesn't make you less of a person than anyone else. To my mind, there is no such thing as being a "normal" person. If you have AS,

I have to break it to you; you're stuck with it. But it doesn't have to be a burden. Besides, being unusual is pretty swell!

WHO DISCOVERED ASPERGER'S SYNDROME?

Asperger's Syndrome is not as new as many people may think. During the Second World War, an Austrian psychiatrist and pediatrician named Hans Asperger took part in a study that examined over four hundred children in a children's hospital. He and a group of doctors studied the social behaviors and interactions of these children.[4]

During his examinations, he observed four boys who acted differently. The four boys' intelligence appeared normal; however, they lacked nonverbal communication skills. According to Dr. Asperger, these kids showed "a lack of empathy, little ability to form friendships, one-sided conversations, intense absorption in a special interest, and clumsy movements."[5]

He also noted that their speaking was either discombobulated, or overly formal, and they spoke on only on one specific topic. He called this "autistic psychopathy." Autistic psychopathy, as defined by Dr. Asperger was a "condition worked by social isolations."[6]

It was originally thought that the children behaved this way because of their isolation in the hospital. He also stated, "Exceptional human beings must be given exceptional educational treatment, treatment which takes into account their special difficulties. Further, we can show that despite abnormality, human beings can fulfill their social role within the community, especially if they find understanding, love and guidance."[7]

Toward the end of World War II, Dr. Asperger, with the help of Sister Victorine, opened up a school for kids who either had autistic psychopathy or had symptoms that were similar to it. He also published his work in Austria.[8]

Before the war ended, the school was bombed in a raid that killed Sister Victorine and destroyed much of Dr. Asperger's work. Presumably, this caused the delay in understanding of the autism spectrum, as well as Asperger's Syndrome, in the West.[9]

In 1981, an English psychiatrist by the name of Dr. Lorna Wing published a series of case studies of children who had shown symptoms similar to those described in Dr. Asperger's past work. She called it "Asperger's Syndrome." Her work became very well known, and in the early 1990s, a description of Asperger's Syndrome was added to several new editions of books on psychiatric disorders. Since then, understanding of AS has grown and evolved.[10]

NEW DISCOVERIES

A few years ago, my mother went to a seminar where a Dr. Volkmar was the keynote speaker. He is a doctor at Yale University and was doing groundbreaking research on autism. He teamed up with a student at MIT and developed something known as "eye tracking." The purpose of this research was to watch and observe subjects in real time as they watched a movie. The movie was *Who's Afraid of Virginia Wolf?* They wore special eye gear while watching this movie.[11]

The eye-tracking system scanned their eyes as they watched the film. They were also hooked up to a CAT-scan, which recorded their brain activity. What he found was absolutely amazing. A part of the brain lit up while the subjects watched this movie.

But in autistic subjects, that part of the brain either didn't "light up," or was missing entirely. Autistic subjects also watched only one thing: the actors' mouths. They never looked at facial expressions. When bored with the movie, their eyes would often wander off and focus on inanimate objects in the room, such as a lamp or picture. Non-autistic people never did that.[12]

This study has offered entire new areas of thought about drug treatment and scientific research to help bring autistic patients "out of their world." The fact that they never looked at the faces of the actors, for instance, opened up a whole new question about how autistic people view the world they live in.

Dr. Volkmar also explained at this seminar that the autistic spectrum is like "a bell-shaped curve." Since there are many disorders in the autistic spectrum, they have been ranked from mildest to more severe. Okay, enough technical stuff.

The best way I can describe the autistic spectrum is that it is like a rainstorm. Imagine that during this rainstorm a bunch of people are hiding under a tree. Depending on where they stand under it, they get wet or not-so-wet. According to this rainstorm analogy, people with

AS are the ones who get the fewest raindrops. AS is among the milder of the disorders of the autistic spectrum, hence it has been called "high-functioning autism."

However, recent studies have shown that this is not so. In fact, there are many differences between AS and what doctors call "classic autism."

People with AS do not exhibit a delay in language or in cognitive development. Either or both of these delays can be seen in people with autism.[13]

People with AS are more aware of and interested in the social world than people with autism. However, this does not change the fact that interaction with others does not come naturally for people with AS. People with autism usually clam up and prefer to be alone.[14]

AS is not usually found in early childhood, as autism is. In fact, some people aren't diagnosed with AS until they're adults.[15]

Many people with AS can adopt strategies to cope with their troubles and are able to live full lives. However, a person with autism is less likely to do so.[16]

Asperger's Syndrome is not a "high-functioning" form of autism. Nonetheless, it is part of the autistic spectrum. If you want more information about Hans Asperger, you can look at the References in the back of this book.

WHAT ARE THE CAUSES OF AS?

Till this day, there is no explanation as to where or how AS originated, but it is widely accepted that there is a hereditary factor. Many doctors believe that multiple genes play a part in causing AS, since the number and severity of symptoms vary so widely among individuals with this diagnosis.[17]

I have read other articles that were written by scientists about the possible causes of Asperger's Syndrome. However, all of them are encoded in scientific terminology. Being only a teen, I don't want to confuse you, since this is not a book about the psychology and science of Asperger's Syndrome. If you're interested in such studies, please see the information sites and books in the References in the back of this book.

Note to Parents: *Treatment*

There is no cure for AS. So don't expect your child to take a prescription drug and be cured the following week or month. It will not happen. But there are things you can do to help your AS child.

The first and most important thing is to be supportive of him. As a devoted parent, you should love your child whether he has AS or not. A person with AS can thrive in life, and it is up to you to make it possible. I probably would not have made it as far as I have without my parents, especially my mom.

Not only should you be supportive, but you should also be a guide in your child's life. She is dependent on you. Be involved with her life, but not obsessively.

Medication is a strong possibility to help with other conditions your child may develop along with AS, such as anxiety, depression, and paranoia. I'm not a pill lover, but I take a few prescriptions, and they help a lot with my depression and other matters.

However, before you even try to put your AS child on any medication, you must have wise counsel from a doctor, for many anti depressants can be harmful both mentally and physically. Years ago, I was put on a drug called Wellbutrin. Instead of it relieving my depression, it made it much worse. I'll elaborate more on this experience later in the book. You must take extreme caution in what medication your AS child takes, for side effects vary with each individual. One drug may be good for one person, but not for another. You might have to experiment a little with different drugs, but only with a doctor's advice.

The other thing I suggest is to have your AS child see a therapist. I know there are many stereotypes of them in movies, but they are actually amazing. I've been seeing a therapist for four years, and it has changed my life dramatically. The therapist I visit every month is my best friend because he not only doesn't judge me, but he also listens to the feelings I express. Therapists are people to talk to, and they help you deal with your problems.

With a therapist, your AS child will have someone to talk to other than you. As a teen with Asperger's Syndrome, there are times I feel it is best to talk to someone other than my parents or other members of my family. I don't know how to explain it, but your AS child may also feel the need to talk to someone else about his troubles.

Note to Parents: *When to Bring the News*

It will not be easy to give your child this kind of news. But before you even tell your child that she has AS, you must receive wise counsel from a doctor. Your child may have some characteristics that are similar to AS, but it doesn't mean that she has Asperger's.

In the year 2000, I was officially diagnosed with Asperger's Syndrome. During my early teens, I started asking questions about why I was so different from everyone else, and my parents answered them by giving me the news that I have AS.

When I asked my parents why they hadn't told me about my AS condition before, they said it was because they didn't want me to feel different than everyone else, or feel that I was *labeled*.

I always felt different than everyone else. I was often called the "weirdo" in school. I did my best not to take such remarks too seriously even though they hurt and often led me to wonder why I was such an oddball. I tried to fit in with my peers but it always led to embarrassing failures because of my strange habits.

Throughout grade school, I would constantly raise my hand whenever the teacher asked the class a question. When she would call on someone else, I would shout out the answer anyway. The other kids would roll their eyes and call me a "know-it-all."

In gym class, I would always duck and cover every time someone threw a ball at me. Everyone would laugh and say things like, "Look at him. He can't catch a ball!"

But when I learned about my AS, it was like a sudden awakening. I no longer had to wonder why I was so different. I did not feel like freak or a retard. I just have a condition to live with.

Your child should know about her AS no matter what. She will reach an age when she will be aware of her differences, and begin asking you questions. This would be a great time to tell your child about her condition.

It would be unwise to tell your child about her condition right after you've learned about it. For one, depending on her age, she might not understand. I always knew I was different, but if my parents had told me that I had AS at eleven, I probably would have been confused.

Another thing that might worry you is how your child might react to this new information. It is not an everyday thing to learn that you have been diagnosed with a neurological disorder.

Your child may be dazed, dejected, or even relieved, but nevertheless she deserves the truth. After you tell her this news, I suggest you encourage her to learn as much about her AS condition as she can, for it may help her to understand it better.

I'm not a doctor, just a smart teenager who knows things from hands-on experiences with AS. Remember, as devoted parents, it is your job not only to love your AS child, but also to look out for her well-being and future interest. Tell her the truth when you feel the time is right; telling her about AS could be an awakening, as it was for me.

Chapter 2

Organization and School

When I was a kid, I used to play with Legos™ and K'NEX™. Before I would start to build, I always sorted all the parts by color. Then I would examine each one to know which piece connected to what.

Since I've developed this "concrete" style of thinking, I'm good with school subjects such as algebra, reading, and history. But when it came to geometry in the tenth grade, I encountered a source of agitation.

Geometry involves thinking on several different levels simultaneously—for instance, finding the lengths of all the lines that make up a three-dimensional triangle. It also sometimes includes trying to imagine a geometric shape rather than seeing it in front of you. This is called *abstract thinking*. There are other topics out there that require abstract thinking, such as religion, biology, and chemistry. I never had trouble comprehending those, but grasping the concepts of geometry was a hassle.

Now, I don't want to scare any of you AS readers who have not taken geometry yet. Solving geometry problems is not a big deal for everyone, for all it requires is to know the steps it takes to solve the lengths, widths, and angles of a problem. Once I learned the different methods and steps it takes to solve a geometry problem, I understood it. It could be a walk in the park; it depends on how you see a problem.

At the high school I went to, geometry was a math class I had to take in order to graduate. This is not a chapter about how to pass geometry, but I have a couple of tips that can be helpful for those of who you are taking or will take this class.

In the past, I've had a tendency to dwell on things, such as being overly concerned with my class grade. It isn't worth giving yourself a heart attack over. If there is a problem that you find confusing, never be afraid to draw and write things out. Then you won't have to worry about trying to remember every little detail of a problem, much less "imagine" it. This has helped me understand and solve geometry problems.

Always ask the teacher for help when you need it. I probably asked half of the questions in my geometry class, and I maintained a ninety-six percent average.

THE NEGATIVE SIDE OF CONCRETE THINKING

I'm such a concrete thinker that I need specific details in order to carry out any given task. A few years ago, I went on a weeklong vacation to Florida with my mom and some relatives. On one of our days there, my aunt told me to sweep the floor. I got out a broom and swept all the dirt and food crumbs into a little pile and walked away, thinking my task was done. A moment later my aunt called me over.

"What is it?" I asked her.

"You didn't finish," she told me.

"Yes I did."

"You didn't clean up the pile."

"You told me to sweep the floor, not to clean it up," I said to her.

Everyone present in the kitchen laughed at me. Even my aunt and mother couldn't resist laughing. I didn't realize anything was wrong.

Another example is when my mom asks me to fetch her purse. A lot of times I don't have a clue where to look for it, so I search throughout the house, running up and down the stairs, looking in each room and nook for it. I could be gone for five or ten minutes before I find it.

I'm a person who needs concrete details in order to accomplish a task. If I don't have specific instructions, I'll most likely do something wrong. What's helped me to avoid such wild goose chases is asking particular questions to either narrow my search, or completely understand what I'm supposed to do with a task.

Whenever my mom tells me to fetch her purse for her, I ask where it is. Then I go to that place, find it, and bring it to her. However, there are times when she doesn't know where her purse is. That's when I have to start my searches. I'll tell you from experience that it is better to ask someone questions to make sure you understand something rather than irritate them by making a mistake.

ORGANIZATION AT SCHOOL

On one particular day in the eighth grade, I was allowed to use a note card with written notes for an upcoming test. Since I always take a test seriously, I took this opportunity and tried to fit as many notes as I could on a note card to help me with the test.

As I walked into class on the day of the test, I realized that I didn't have the note card with me. I sat my books on my desk and ran to my locker, tearing through it, trying to find this silly note card. When I couldn't find it, I panicked. *What was I going to do?* I kept wondering. *I'm going to flunk this test! I can't take an F!*

I then called my mom, who was at work, and begged her to go home and get the note card for me. Thankfully, she was able to leave work and get this ridiculous note card so I could do the test. What I should have done was properly study for the test rather than rely totally on some notes on a note card.

In any case, I do not suggest that you call your parents when they're at work because you forgot something for school. This would show your parents that you lack responsibility. My mother had quite a temper with me. To avoid such unpleasantness, always be prepared and organized.

What has helped me a lot in organizing for my classes is having different binders and folders for each school subject. Then I would color-code and label them.

When it comes to deciding whether to use binders or folders to store subject- assignments, I recommend binders. Binders may be bulkier, but because of that, they can store more assignments throughout a school year versus a folder. Folders also have the tendency of falling and breaking apart more easily than binders.

I strongly suggest you use dividers in your binders or folders. For all my classes, I have at least three dividers in each of my binders, labeled as "notes," "tests," and "assignments." I not only break up my assignments in these dividers, but I also place them in the order of the dates that I finished them.

For the days you're missing school, I suggest that you have another binder or folder for assignments that you have to make up. Then you won't have to worry about missing any of them.

My last suggestion for keeping yourself organized and ready for school is to have either a crayon box or a utensil pouch. I prefer the utensil pouch because I felt a crayon box to be a bit childish in middle and high school. A utensil pouch is also lighter, smaller and has as much room as a crayon box.

In my utensil pouch, I always have a few lead pencils, a highlighter, a calculator, and a few of my other little possessions. With a pouch, I never had to worry about losing a pencil, or misplacing any other utensil. It may sound like a lot of work, but it has its benefits.

Note to Parents: *IEPs and Aides*

You may have to arrange some modifications with the school so that your AS child can have a great and successful time there. My mother has set up an Individual Education Plan (IEP) for me every year since kindergarten. An IEP can help your AS kid on a variety of levels, including extra educational aid, and behavioral modifications.

This is very important, parents. When you're looking for schools for your AS kid to attend, make sure the one you choose has aides or teachers who can help special needs students. Depending on your AS child, he may need to have a lot of modifications in his IEP.

The other thing that may be helpful for your AS kid is to have an aide or interventionalist in the classes he is in. Aides can help your child understand the class material better, as well as help with many other things. However, having an aide present in the classroom with your AS kid can lead to bullying.

Back in the eighth grade, I had an aide help me out with science. Because I had an aide following me around in a classroom with twenty or thirty other students, I felt embarrassed. Several of the kids in the class would look at me awkwardly and giggle.

The aide saw this, and began to act like a second teacher, helping everyone in the room, rather than just me. The giggling and awkward glances ended, and everyone seemed to forget that I had an aide present. I would introduce this thought to your AS kid's aide.

Also make sure your AS child's aide is a person he can get along with. In the eighth grade, I had two aides. The one who helped me with science was a very nice lady, but the man who helped me with my other issues was not a pleasant person to be around. He was grouchy, mean, and uninterested in me or in understanding my diagnosis. You don't want that kind of individual to be around your AS child.

TEACHERS

I've had mostly great teachers, but I also had some that I view as mean. In the eighth grade, I had a science teacher who I felt abhorred me as soon as I walked into her class. Not only did she have disdain for *me*, but also for the rest of the class. She shouted all the time, and instead of teaching the class, she had all the students work in groups.

I know it's a common thing to work in groups for a science lab, but the teacher did not even explain the material we were using. I'll get into more details about this story later on in the book.

What has helped me get along with many of my teachers was bonding with them. In the seventh grade, I had an English teacher who loved movies. I'm quite the movie addict myself, and because of our common interest in movies, we got along very well. Reach out to your teachers. See if there are any interests that you share with them. It may sound a little odd, but because I developed friendships with my teachers I had a better time in their classrooms.

How you get along with a teacher depends on how well you learn from his class. You need to know your teacher, as well as how he teaches the class. If a teacher doesn't get involved with the class or doesn't explain things very well, then talk to your parents and other school staff about it. They'll know what to do.

Note to Parents: *Teachers*

You have to be considerate when it comes to teachers. There are many decent teachers out there, but there are also some you may not want your

AS child to be around. Now I'm not trying to sound harsh, but there are some teachers who are hardheaded, arrogant, and even mean.

The teacher that you should not have teaching your AS kid is someone who is overly strict, unwilling to learn about your child's condition, and a control freak. It's always good that a teacher is in control of the room, but when a teacher abuses that power by being too strict, they can even be perceived as bullying. Your AS child probably wouldn't fit in with that kind of personality.

Another type of teacher you don't want to have your AS child around is one who doesn't teach the class or maintain law and order over it. I once had a teacher who was very informative and good at explaining things, but she had no control of the class. It would get so crazy that kids would shout at each other across the room and even shoot spit wads and throw paper airplanes. As a person with Asperger's Syndrome, I could not focus in that kind of classroom environment.

A THOUGHT, PARENTS

For many years, my mom would talk to the school principal and ask to meet my teachers before the new school year started. She would meet them, talk with them, and give them some information about my Asperger's Syndrome. Then my mom would bring me along afterwards and I would meet my new teachers a few weeks before school started. With this arrangement, I got a chance to meet my teachers ahead of time.

This kind of meeting was easy to set up in my elementary school since there were only six teachers for each grade level. But starting with middle school and into high school, it grew challenging because there were more teachers, usually two or three for each subject in each grade.

With the school principal's permission, my mom sat in on the teachers' classes. This way she knew how they taught the class, treated their students, and what the classroom's environment was like. If you have the time, I strongly suggest you do this.

However, there may be some teachers who won't allow you to observe their class. One time a teacher got very mouthy with my mom about her coming into the class and observing it while she taught. I did not end up in that teacher's class.

I don't want to jump to conclusions, but when a teacher doesn't allow you to come into her class and observe while she teaches, most likely that person wouldn't be fit for your AS child. There are teachers who are great at their jobs, but some may not like the idea of someone outside of the school administration observing his class.

Nonetheless, if someone does get defensive about this matter, I think it would be best not to place your AS kid in that individual's class.

The teacher you want instructing your AS child is someone who is fun, open-minded, willing to learn about your AS kid, but is also stern and knowledgeable. How well your child learns a subject always depends on how good the teacher is.

Note to Parents: *Classrooms*

After you meet a teacher, you need to examine her classroom. Classrooms can vary from being cramped to being open-spaced. They can also be very noisy and disorganized when twenty to thirty kids are all in one room.

If the room is cramped, it wouldn't be a good idea for your AS child to attend that class. I've been in classrooms where there wasn't much room, and that were overly flooded with students. As a person with AS, I like to have space around me. If I don't have enough space, I get overwhelmed. If you run into a situation where the teacher you pick for your AS child is in a cramped room, you will have to improvise.

That's when specific seat selections come in handy. It is best to have your AS child sit in the front row, either near the teacher's desk or on either end of the front row.

Sitting in the center of a classroom is not a good idea.

In my eighth grade math class, the teacher assigned seats by students' last names, alphabetically. Since my last name is in the middle of the alphabet, I ended up in the center of the classroom. Every day in that classroom, I felt like I was sitting in a crowded shopping mall, with people constantly chit-chatting around me. With all that commotion from the other students, I couldn't concentrate on what the teacher was saying when she stood in the front of the class.

I'm not saying that your AS kid has trouble with concentration, but with such noises around him, he will be less likely to focus in class. That's why I suggest the front row—because it's away from the distracting noises. Also, sitting somewhere in the middle of the classroom or away from the teacher can lead to a classmate bullying your AS child. Setting up this little arrangement with your AS kid's teachers can avoid those types of issues. I also suggest that you have your AS kid sit at the desk next to the teacher's. I always felt more secure when I was near the teacher. Your AS child may feel the same way.

There may be times where one of your AS child's teachers decides to organize the classroom's desks differently throughout the school year. My eighth-grade Language Arts teacher changed our seats and desk positions often. In one of the positions, he had our desks arranged in an oval shape. If something like this does happen, talk to the teacher, and make sure your AS child is in one of the front ends or is sitting near the teacher.

The last thing I suggest is to never have your AS child change seats. After I sit in the same seat for a while, I get comfortable and attached to sitting at it. But when I have to suddenly change my seat for another one, it is hard for me to adapt to the new spot and view of the classroom. Most people with AS have a difficulty with transitioning. Keep that in mind with your AS kid.

TESTS

Tests are unpredictable, stressful, and in many cases (especially in high school) hard and tricky. Nevertheless, there are ways to make them less of a challenge. Throughout my school years, I have developed strategies to assist me in test taking.

With any test you are to take, you'll need some supplies, which may vary according to the subject of the test. When I was in Algebra II, a graphing calculator was required, and sometimes a piece of scrap paper.

Your teacher should go over the supplies you'll need for the tests, as well as for the class. For any test, always have a pencil with a good eraser.

Whatever you do, don't rush through a test. Take your time, and check your answers over. If you are confused about how a question is worded, do not be afraid to reread or rewrite it in a way that makes sense to you. If you don't know the answer to a question, I suggest you place a period or circle by the question you have not answered, move on to the other questions, and come back to it later.

If you find valuable information in a problem, underline the details that strike you as important, and then write them down either on an open space on the test or on a separate sheet of paper. Never feel embarrassed to ask the teacher for aid. He may not be able to give you the answer, but he can certainly assist you.

In some instances when I've taken a test, some kids like looking over a person's test to copy their answers down. To prevent this, I suggest using a separate sheet of blank paper to cover your answers while taking a test. This has also helped my eyes to focus on one problem at a time, rather than drift over the test's questions and get confused about which one to answer.

In the past, when I have not finished a test, I would approach my teacher and tell him that I wasn't done with it. Since I'm in an IEP, and one of its modifications is having extended time to take tests, my teacher would take the test and allow me to finish it later. Tests can be intimidating and stressful, but they don't have to be your worst nightmare.

DO NOT CHEAT!

Cheating is not the right way to go. I admit that I have cheated on tests a couple of times. In the seventh grade, I had to take a test in world history. The night before the test I was busy and didn't get a lot of studying done.

When my seventh-bell class came around the next day, I entered my world history class and looked over my notes as much as I could before the teacher began handing out the test. As he started passing out the test, I placed my books on the floor and began to take it, answering the questions as best as I could.

When there was only ten minutes left of the class, I had answered only half of the questions. *I couldn't get a bad grade on a test. I needed to hold onto my A for the class,* I thought. I looked down at my books and folders that were next to my foot on the floor. Quickly, I shuffled through my folders, found my notes, placed them on top of my stack of books, and looked at them as I tried to answer the questions I left blank. I did the best I could not to be seen.

A minute before the bell rang, I handed in the test, feeling relieved that I had finished it, and I hoped that neither the teacher nor anyone else had seen me. The following day, my history teacher called me into his room.

He asked me, "Did you cheat on the test?"

I could not lie to him. "Yes."

A look of disappointment crossed his face.

"I thought you were a better student than that," he said to me. "You get a zero on the test."

The zero damaged my grade. I was lucky to bring my class grade up to a low B. In addition, it took me awhile to regain his trust. Never cheat on a test. It brings many negative consequences.

Make sure you study for every test you take. If you don't get enough time to prepare and study for a test, tell your teacher that you're not ready for the test and you need more time for preparation. If you feel rushed when taking a test, walk up to the teacher and tell him that you're not finished and that you need to wrap it up later.

Note to Parents: Tests

Be on alert when your AS child takes a test. After she takes one, ask how she felt about it. As an individual with AS, how well I do on a test depends on how it is set up. Now your AS child may not do well on a test because she didn't study well or freaked over it, but you may have to work with your child's teachers about some accommodations.

In the sixth grade, I had a test in which all the questions were crammed onto one page. The questions were so compressed together that I couldn't tell what answer I was giving to which question. I failed the test.

When I had to take it a second time to increase my grade, my mom told my teacher to make all the questions bigger so I could see them clearly. The test ended up being three pages long rather than just one, but I aced it.

In the fifth grade, I had a weekly math test that I always aced. About halfway through the year, the test paper went from the normal white to a bright pink. I couldn't read the test because of the intensity of the bright color, and I ended up flunking it.

In my ninth-grade English class, I was given a five- to ten-minute range to take my vocabulary tests. I felt pressured and stressed whenever I had to take a vocabulary test, because I felt I never had enough time to finish them. In addition, the classroom was cramped. Twenty students in a room that should have housed probably no more than fifteen made me feel uncomfortable and less able to concentrate.

If your AS child is not the cause of his failing the tests, then approach and talk to your child's teachers about some changes they may have to make regarding how the tests are set up. Make sure all your child's tests have readable text. You may also want to ask that all the tests he takes be on white paper, or a shade that he can read the writing on. Various shades may affect your AS child's eyes and ability to read or focus.

Allow extended time on tests for your Asperger's child so he doesn't feel pressured into finishing it in a limited amount of time. When your child takes a test, have him take it in a quiet room, like the IEP room, with an aide. Not only will he be able to concentrate better, but he can also get some help if needed. And lastly, prohibit pop quizzes for your child. Always have at least a three-day notice so your AS child can have the time he needs to study.

A BRIEF VIEW ON HOMEWORK

As an individual with Asperger's Syndrome, homework was never an issue for me. I generally get it done and turned in on time. But homework can be stressful, particularly studying for a test, or working on a big research project. After a seven- to eight-hour day at school, I want to go home and relax, but homework is unavoidable.

It gets harder and heavier the further you get in school. When I hit high school, I stopped asking my parents for help with homework, because the material I was learning was beyond them.

To get the help I needed with my classes, I often went to school a little early so I could get my teachers' help before class started. If I needed to, I would stay after school. The best help you can get is from your teachers. They know the material best. That's why I try to get most of my homework done at school, so I won't be confused on how to do it at home.

If you're confused about an assignment, never be afraid to ask for help and, if need be, stay after school for a day to get the help you need. You may also want to add some modifications regarding homework to your IEP, or special helps, such as extended time.

Chapter 3

Transitioning

At the start of my freshman year in high school, it was difficult trying to locate classrooms. Compared to middle school, which was a single-floor building in a rectangular shape; the high school was two-story building that was very easy to get lost in. In order to get to each class without tardiness, I had to run from one floor to the other, carrying with me my books and binders for four or five different classes.

It was quite a load, and the hallways were incredibly packed with other students. Trying to get through the hallways was like trying to get through a traffic jam. Whenever I went through one of those congested hallways, I felt my private space was being invaded. It was so tight that it was difficult to breathe, with everyone knocking into me, and all the people touching me. I dreaded every day of it. I had to get out of those situations. I could no longer take high school.

After a week of this, I walked out the school's front door to cool off. This was a warning sign to the school and my parents that I needed help. With the care and guidance of my parents, I was relieved from school for a couple of weeks to get the proper treatment I needed, which gave my parents the time to set up my IEP and a better schedule for my classes.

From this experience I learned that, whether I liked it or not, everything changes, and the future is at best unpredictable. With Asperger's Syndrome, I like to keep things regular and afloat. I am also an individual who has to know about things ahead of time.

Going from middle school to high school disrupted my relaxed school attitude. I wasn't used to the high school, and there were seven different classroom environments. It's nearly impossible to adapt to all of them, especially when the bell rings for the next class.

In the elementary days, I had a much different schedule than high school. I had only one teacher and one classroom. I didn't have to worry about having to meet several different teachers and attend different classrooms. It was much easier for me to learn from one teacher rather than seven. I also didn't have to worry about running through the hallways to get to class on time.

Having only a single class all day long seems like a pleasant dream, but unfortunately, the older you are and the longer you are in school, the more classrooms and teachers you'll have.

In any stressful situation, *do not flee from school.* Evading your problems only worsens them. When I fled school in the ninth grade, I nearly created a mass panic. That is the last thing you want to do. Because I took that rash action, not only were my parents deeply concerned, but

I was also put on school alert. My teachers had their eyes on me like a hawk for that school year to make sure I didn't leave the room.

If you ever feel down or overwhelmed, it is best to get help. Talk to your school guidance counselor to help get the stress off your chest. Since I have an IEP, an interventionalist is assigned to me. I always felt comfortable talking to her about my troubles.

The ninth grade was not my best school year, but the further I got into it, the more it improved. Never be afraid to sit down with an aide, an interventionalist, or even a guidance counselor for assistance. They're there for you.

If you are attending a school that is architecturally a maze, try to set up your schedule in such a way that most of your classes are near each other. If the school you attend has two or more floors, see if you can have all your classes on one floor. My parents made this arrangement for my freshman year, and that made it much easier for me to get around the building.

With the issue involving class changes, my parents set up a plan where I was allowed to leave each class a few minutes early so I could go to my locker and exchange books and binders for the next class without having to be in the hallway traffic. This way I was able to get to each class on time, and I didn't have to carry five sets of books at once. If you have trouble getting to your classes on time, I suggest you talk to your aide or interventionalist, as well as your teachers, about this plan.

If any teacher doesn't allow you this extra leniency, get your parents involved. Some teachers I have come across have been a bit intolerant about having their students leave class early.

Note to Parents: *Helping with School Transition*

When your child transitions from one school to another, I suggest you and your child familiarize yourselves with the new school before the year begins. Walk around in the hallways; make your AS child familiar with the building. Learn where his or her classrooms, the cafeteria, gymnasium, etcetera, are located. I did this with my mom at every school I went to before the new school-year started, except for the ninth grade, because the school didn't open until the day before class started.

I didn't have enough time to get acquainted with the school staff as well as the building. Always make sure your AS child is organized ahead of time so she won't be flustered during the first few weeks of school. That is not a great way to start a school year, and I know this from the ninth grade.

VACATION BREAKS

Another transition issue I always have is the change between the school year to vacation and back again. My three chunks of vacation from school are Christmas time, Easter break, and summer vacation. Of the three vacations, summer is the hardest for me.

Most kids I know can't wait for vacation, especially summer break. It is the time to totally relax and be a goofball. When school is out for summer vacation break, I'm being pulled away from a working environment, and thrown into a long period of time with nothing to do. I feel morose, for I wonder what to do with a couple of month's time off.

I always try to find something worthwhile to do in my time off, but trying to commit myself to something without the proper motivation that school work can bring through due dates and points can be difficult. Something that isn't too productive, like playing video games or watching a load of movies, often distracts me.

After a month of such a pattern, I begin to get used to the long time I have off. By the time I finally accept summer break, I realize that there are only a few weeks left, and I grow dejected.

An acquaintance of mine at school told me that it's better to be bored than to do school work. I can understand his point, but I'm a person who just has to do something. On one of my summer breaks, I tried to write a fantasy story. I had planned out all the events, side plots, and characters that would be in it before break started, yet I could not motivate myself to sit in front of a computer and type. As the summer break ended, I felt that I had wasted it on my personal amusement instead of focusing on writing.

There's nothing wrong with enjoying your vacation time. I don't want to give the impression that I don't like vacation; in fact, I actually enjoy time off. After a while, though, I feel exhausted by it. If I don't do something that I find worthy of my time, I get upset.

It is up to you how you spend your vacation. Do whatever you want. If you ever get bored over your summer break or any other vacation, look for a job, or do volunteer work. Do a school assignment if one is given. For my ninth grade Advanced English class, I had to read two books over break. Rather than waiting for the last week I had off, I began reading them a few weeks into my break. In any case, do what you want. As my Mom always tells me, "You should enjoy your vacation time while it lasts."

It can be quite a pain when school starts again. I am transitioned from a time of boredom and relaxation, and thrust once again into tight schedules, crowded hallways and classrooms and, of course, tests and exams.

In order to be prepared for the start of a new school year, I have to reset my routine from sleeping in till nine or ten o'clock in the morning to waking up at six or seven. And the worst part about it is having to go to bed early (since my parents enforce a curfew for my bedtime at nine o'clock on the school evenings). I also have to restart the drills of preparing myself in the morning, such as taking care of personal hygiene, eating breakfast, and getting to school. These are not easy to do.

Before the school year starts, it is best to get back into the routine of the tasks you do in the morning and at night. I always prepare myself early, a week before school starts, so I can adapt to the new schedule. I know it is a challenge to get readapted to school, but it is best to get a head start rather than wait till the last night before the first day of school.

If sleep is an issue for you, you may want to keep to the schedule of getting up and going to bed earlier. I never did this because I always liked going to bed late and sleeping in.

WEATHER CHANGES

Each season affects me differently. In the spring and fall, I develop horrible allergies. Winter is typically cold, and it happens to be the time of year when I usually get ill. And summer, well, I'll just say it is hot and dry. Not everyone likes it cold or hot and I have met no one who enjoys allergies. But weather changes can also affect people mentally and emotionally.

When spring and summer arrive, I feel giddy with the warmer temperatures, and the sight of puffy white clouds and sunshine. During autumn and winter, I am overcome with the thought of snow. But since the sixth grade, I have viewed autumn and winter as a time of melancholy. The trees look dead, the coldness of the weather is bitter, and school tends to grow more challenging, especially with the start of the long third quarter that starts after Christmas break.

A heavy workload and a bitterly cold season is not a good combination. It's fair to say I'm one of the many people who just love the sun. Most people I know prefer summer to winter, but when winter weather comes, I grow sad. My psychiatrist calls this Seasonal Depression. He told me that Seasonal Depression is an emotional disorder that is triggered by the lack of sunlight. It is a widely known disorder that usually hits people during the seasons of autumn and winter.

If you feel dejected during a certain season, particularly winter, you should talk to your doctor about your mood change. This does not necessarily mean that you have Seasonal Depression. It's normal to have mood swings from time to time, but if it's recurring at a specific time of year, you should definitely seek some help.

I was never prescribed any new medication for Seasonal Depression, but the dosages of some of my pills were increased. This helped a little, but not a whole lot. Instead, I found other ways to fight through it. One contribution that helped me get through Seasonal Depression was transferring to a vocational school in my junior year of high school.

The hallways weren't tightly packed. The school was a one-story building. The classrooms were easier to find. I also got along with the staff and other students better than at my previous high school.

In addition, the school I transferred to offered me a chance to get a head start in learning the career that I want to pursue in Digital Design. Because of that opportunity, I'm learning about something that I enjoy. See if you can incorporate a class that involves something that you like, whether it is a lab like I.T., Digital Design, or even Graphic Design. You can also look for other elective classes that may interest you, such as woodshop, creative writing, or a computer class.

Note to Parents: *Helping with Weather Change*

There are different ways you can help your AS child if she feels down during a certain season. One possibility that may be unlikely is moving somewhere closer to the equator. Some people I know who have Seasonal Depression have moved to Florida. Since they've moved there, they haven't had any trouble. I do not suggest this unless you're getting a job transfer nearer to the equator. But if this opportunity ever comes around, and if your AS child gets depressed during the winter, it could be an option.

Medication is always a possibility. It may do the trick, but as I've cautioned before, use pills only with a doctor's permission. Some meds can be helpful, but others can be harmful.

One thing that my psychiatrist suggested was buying a specific lamp. He explained to me that when turned on, it gives off colorful lights, making the person with Seasonal Depression feel they're in a happy and warmer climate. This is called *lamp therapy.*

According to research I read on lamp therapy, there are certain chemicals in the brain called neurotransmitters, which create endorphins. Endorphins bring exhilarating emotions such as happiness.[1] One of its several triggers is the sun's light. If you take that away, it shuts the neurotransmitters down, which limits the happiness a person can feel. Light therapy tricks the mind since the lamp's light simulates sunlight, making a person with Seasonal Depression feel happy.[2]

I never bought this lamp because I would have had to get up much earlier in the morning to sit in front of the lamp for forty-five minutes. I could have done it during the evening, but my psychiatrist told me that it would be better to turn the lamp on at the start of the day. The idea of turning it on in the morning was so I would feel happy throughout the day rather than just in the late afternoon or evening.

I'm not a morning person; I enjoy my sleep too much. But this lamp therapy may help your AS child. It is worth a try.

If your AS child is under a lot of pressure and is depressed at school, it might be wise for her to take a day off. Having a day off always cleared my mind of the stresses that school can bring.

Fleeing from a problem isn't good, but taking a break isn't a crime, either. This does not mean your AS child should miss a day every week, nor should it become a habit. That only makes matters worse. Absences can tally up and assignments can be missed if your AS child misses too much school. If you do decide to let him take a day off, I suggest that you tell him to go to his classes and get the assignments he will miss so he can work on them at home.

I'm not a fan of homework, but when I'm put under stress, I tend to work best when I am at home. Do not let your AS kid play or goof off until all of his assignments are done. I learned this the hard way a few years ago. I spent a mental-health day video gaming rather than catching up on my schoolwork.

When I got back to school the next day, my teachers were expecting me to turn in my assignments, but I had none to give them. Do not allow your AS child to play around during the day he has off. Make sure the work is done first—before allowing any leisure time.

If there are some assignments that your AS kid can't get from teachers, call the interventionalist and teachers, and tell them that your child will be gone for the day and that they should gather all the assignments, so your student can finish them later. This is a good way to make sure your AS kid doesn't fall behind in school.

At the school I go to, there's only a certain number of days I can miss before penalties arise. Include in your AS child's IEP that it is permitted to have occasional "mental health days." I've never known what those penalties are, but with mental health days incorporated in my IEP, it has helped me to avoid them.

You should also require permission for your AS child to phone you. When I am under stress, I feel the most comfortable in talking to my mom or dad.

If your AS child happens to call you when she is in the middle of school and says she can't make it through the day, you might have to pick her up. But before you make that decision, talk to her and try to relax her. You can try to negotiate with her to stay through the day. But if your child says she just can't make it through the day, then pick her up.

If you are unable to pick her up from school, tell her to stay on the line and try to get hold of someone you know to learn if that person can pick her up. When my parents couldn't pick me up, my mom always called my grandfather to come and get me. Call a family member or a close friend that your AS child will feel comfortable around.

If you can't find someone who can pick your child up, then you'll probably have to tell your child you can't. Don't be tactless on the phone. If you are calm and gentle, your AS child will feel less anxious and may be able to make it through the day.

Chapter 4

Sensitive Senses

There is an ocean's worth of information about the sensory problems of people with Asperger's Syndrome—in books and articles, at retail stores and on the Internet, but I feel it is worth mentioning based on my experiences as a person with AS. I have a bit of a different sensory issue compared to a lot of people that I know, and I think it's important to share these experiences.

SIGHT

Sight isn't too much of a deal for me, but I do have difficulty with some colors, specifically with neon colors like fire-engine red, or hot pink. The intensity of these colors makes me want to close my eyes. If I stare at such a color for a while, I will develop a headache. I briefly mentioned in Chapter Two that all the assignments and tests I take are to be on white paper. Well, this is the reason why.

In the sixth grade, I had to buy note cards for a research project. Part of my project grade was writing the information I had obtained from my resources onto note cards. My teacher suggested that I use colored note cards to help separate the different resources I had to use for my project.

Taking into account my teacher's advice, I went to a store with my mom after dinner to buy some note cards. It ended up that all the colored note cards were bright shades of flamingo pink and mustard yellow.

My mom asked me, "Can you read and write notes on these note cards?"

Not in the mood for shopping on a school night, I said, "Yes."

So we bought the note cards. The next day, when I tried to write down my notes on the note cards, I could not even glance at them. Right after school, I told my mom that I had a difficulty with them. We then went shopping to find colored note cards that I could read and write on. After going to several different stores, we decided to just go with white note cards.

The next day, my mom explained to my teacher that I could not work with colored note cards. Since then, my mom has given my teachers specific instructions that, whether it was a research project or another school assignment, I was to work only on white paper.

In addition to bright colors, I have trouble with dark colors. A while ago I saw a movie about the Vietnam War called *Apocalypse Now*. It was a superb film, but much of it took place either at night or in dark locations. There's no doubt that this gave a very eerie feeling to the film, but the colors were so dark that I couldn't tell what was happening during most of the movie.

I don't know if this was the director's intention, but I could have seen the film better if I had worn a pair of night-vision goggles. The bottom line is that some people with AS have difficulty with colors. I'm not trying to say that you have this difficulty; many non-AS people also have problems with colors. I knew a kid in high school who was color-blind. He told me he couldn't drive because it was hard for him to tell the difference between the red and green lights at intersections.

Colors can affect people differently. If a certain color does bother you, for instance a shade on an assignment, tell your teacher that it bothers you and that you can't finish or even do it. Then request to have your assignments either on white paper or on a color that doesn't bother your eyes.

HEARING

Blaring music, people yelling, fire alarms, sirens, and fireworks, among other things, create a vast amount of noise. Bang! Ka-boom! Thud! Thunk! Crash! Splash! Noise! Noise! Noise! It overwhelms me like a crushing tidal wave. Every time I encounter a noisy event, whether it is a school assembly or a theater, I cover my ears and run to the nearest exit.

Back in kindergarten, I was originally part of a play. Due to the combination of the loud singing and the thought of standing on a stage in front of hundreds of adults, I panicked and ran away screaming. I never liked to stand before a crowd of people or be in the midst of a chaotic event that involves an overload of noise. I cannot tolerate it.

At the convention my mom went to, which I mentioned in the first chapter, Dr. Volkmar spoke of the four places a person with Asperger's

Syndrome would not feel comfortable going to at school: the cafeteria, gymnasium, playground/recess, and the auditorium.

Each of these locations is built to hold a lot of people, which can lead to much disorganization and noise. People with AS prefer quiet and controlled environments. That's why I never went to school events that took place in any of those locations. I just can't stand the noise. Both my parents and teachers had to twist my arm in order to make me go to such noisy events. Sometimes it worked, but most of the time it didn't.

Areas outside of school that I was never comfortable with were malls, theaters, circuses, and sports stadiums. When I was five, my parents took me to an IMAX Theater to see a movie. As soon as the Surround Sound came on, I wailed and covered my ears. My parents had to drag me out of the theater.

I also had trouble with mechanical instruments that make a lot of noise, like lawn mowers, motorcycles, and vacuum cleaners. Whenever my mom started the vacuum cleaner, I would immediately stick my fingers in my ears, run into my room, and slam the door shut.

There's a reason for my inability to handle noise. I've always thought that it was just a characteristic of my AS. To some degree that is true, but a few years ago I found a more in-depth reason that some people cannot bear high noise levels.

On PBS, I saw a science study about eardrums and how they can be affected by sound. This study said the eardrum can withstand only a certain amount of noise before it reaches an "overload." At that point, the eardrum reacts, causing the person to cover their ears or, as with me, to scream and have the urge to flee from the scene.

If nothing is done to stop the noise or if the person doesn't get away from it, the noise can cause severe damage to the eardrums, which can lead to deafness. This sensitivity to noise varies with each individual. With AS I am more sensitive to noise than most, and I get easily overwhelmed by it.

The unfortunate thing is that most noises are beyond my control. The only time I enjoy loudness is when it's in my control, like listening to a great music piece. Whenever I hear the classical music piece "Carmina Burana," I always crank up the volume on my stereo. Since "Carmina Burana" is something I like, I don't mind going beyond my comfort zone in turning up the volume.

The only other noise I have come to enjoy is "white noise." White noise is usually neither loud nor rhythmic, but calm, like the waves of the ocean, or a steady rainfall. To help me sleep at night, I always have a fan running. The unvarying sounds make me calm enough to fall asleep, and it helps circulate cool air in my room. It has been a beneficial relaxant.

COPING WITH NOISE

When I was a child, noises affected me a lot. However, as I got older, I could tolerate them better. I now go to theaters and I no longer have to cover my ears whenever my mom turns on the vacuum cleaner. But I still won't attend school assemblies that involve a lot of blaring instruments and cheering crowds.

It all depends on you. If you can handle loud noises, that's fine. If not, avoid them. If there's an occasion where you have to go to a noisy event, like a birthday party, you might want to bring earplugs. It may sound silly, but back when I started going to movie theaters, I always brought earplugs with me in case it got too loud. I knew I couldn't turn the theater's volume down with a remote, as I do my television, but I had a back-up plan just in case the noise got overwhelming.

I eventually outgrew the need for earplugs, and I can now handle loud noises better. It all depends on how your comfort zone is set with noise levels. You may or may not grow out of it, and there are many different kinds of noises. Some can affect you differently than others.

If you do feel ready to sit through a noisy event, then give it a try. When I was seven, I tried to go to a basketball game. As soon as the scoreboards rang and the masses shouted, I couldn't handle it. I told my dad that I could not stand it even with my earplugs in place. We left the bleachers and went upstairs to watch the game from the concession stands. I then knew that I couldn't handle blaring noises, but I felt good because I had at least tried it. There's nothing wrong with trying; you'll only benefit from it.

Note to Parents: How to Help Your AS Kid with Noise

When you want your AS child to participate in a noisy event, talk to her about it. If she is persistent about not wanting to go to such an event, try to persuade her in a polite way.

That may sound hard, but it worked with me on several occasions.

When I was eight, the movie *101 Dalmatians* came to theaters. Since I was a Walt Disney addict, I wanted to see it, but the thought of being in a movie theater frightened me. My parents persuaded me not to think about the noise but to keep my focus on the screen. In addition, my parents made sure I had my earplugs with me as a backup. "Think of it as a big TV," my mom told me once we got to the theater. "It won't hurt you."

I ended up having a great time. I sat through the whole movie without even using my earplugs. By the age of nine, I went to movie theaters every chance I had. After a while, I did not need my earplugs, but I always had them as backup. There have been some occasions, though, when the Surround Sound was too loud.

For instance, my mom and I went to see *Star Wars: The Phantom Menace*. I had never experienced a movie that was so loud; I could feel my chest vibrate. Even my mom couldn't sit through it. We got up and left when the commercials were still going.

If the noise of an event is too much for your AS kid, get her out of there. You don't want her to suffer through a noisy event like an overly loud movie. It's not a pleasant experience. Even though my mom and I were only in the theater for five minutes, my ears were ringing the entire drive home.

Note to Parents: *Fire Drills and Other School Events*

In elementary school, as soon as the alarm bell started ringing, I would instantly plug my fingers in my ears and screech at the top of my lungs. You don't want your AS child to go through this kind of hysteria. Try to get at least a week's notice before a fire or a tornado drill is scheduled. With an early notice, she will at least be prepared for it.

Drills are unavoidable and are required at every school. There also may be times when the fire drill goes off by accident, or unexpectedly, as the result of a foolish prank. I suggest you teach your AS child ways to cope with the noise so she will not go haywire when it occurs. My mom always told me to cover my ears and stay by the teacher. I always felt safer when I was close to the teacher during a drill.

If there happens to be a school event like a pep rally or a band parade, again, request a week's notice from the school so it'll give your AS child time to prepare for it and decide whether she wants to go to it or not.

In case I didn't want to go to such an event, my mom set up a plan— I could go to the principal's office to work on assignments or read a book during the event. Make this a possibility. With this plan, I never felt pressured into having to go to a loud assembly, and I also had some alone time to catch up on assignments and relax.

MY PICKY TASTES

For years, I would eat only Goldfish crackers, peas, ice cream, cake, grilled cheese, and Cheerios (without the bowl of milk). Of the foods

I limited myself to, grilled cheese and Cheerios were number one. I always begged my parents to make me Cheerios for breakfast and grilled cheese for lunch and dinner.

Whenever my parents introduced me to something new to eat, I would go through a step-by-step food analysis. First, I would pick it up tenderly and then look at it. Next, I'd pull it slowly to my nose and sniff it. Then I would take the tiniest bite of it and swish it around my mouth. If I liked it, I'd finish eating it. If I didn't like it, I pushed it aside.

I grew out of this habit by the time I was eleven. By that time, I no longer ate just grilled cheese and Cheerios. I can't tell you what you want to eat. If you like a particular food, then go for it. But do your best in trying to find something new. Experiment. There's always something different out there to eat and savor.

Note to Parents: *What Can You Do to Help Your AS Kid Be Less Picky?*

There's not a whole lot I can suggest as to how to make your AS child eat his green beans. This is a common thing for most kids, but my little food analysis is rare, compared to the norm. If I did not like the food I was served, my parents told me to eat it, and I would obey even if I had to grimace or put a clothespin on my nose. If your AS child isn't cooperative, you might have to find some other methods to make him eat his veggies. Whichever strategy you take, make sure that it does not involve anger. Anger will only make you the enemy. You'll have to be patient.

SMELLS AND SCENTS

There's not much I can say about the sense of smell. As an individual with Asperger's Syndrome, I feel the same about smelling things as any other person. But I do have certain peculiar interests in different scents.

When I was four, my parents and I moved to a new house. Often we would visit furniture and carpet stores. Every time we went into those stores, my nose would come alive, and I'd sniff out the place due to the varying scents the carpet gave off. I would be lost in the store for minutes.

My parents would often later find me sprawled out on a bed of fresh new carpet. There is nothing necessarily wrong with a certain interest in a scent, just so long as it is not a dominating factor.

HAVING MY SPACE

I don't mean to fool you with this subheading; this section is not about the Internet site, MySpace. This is about having personal space around you. When I walk or sit at a table, I like to have some room around me. Having personal space is like having boundaries. I need boundaries between me and other people to feel comfortable. When I feel a person is too close to me, it makes me feel very insecure.

I dislike being touched even more. Whenever someone pats me on the back or on the shoulder, I recoil. I get overwhelmed when my space is invaded. In the past, I've even gotten hostile.

One time, in a lunch line in grade school, a kid stood very close behind me. I felt quite uneasy about it so I moved a little forward toward the kid in front of me. When the line started to move again, he reached out and poked me in the back.

I jumped probably a yard from where I stood and shouted, "What do you want?"

It wasn't until I was nine that I would finally allow a limited number of people to touch me. As I've mentioned in earlier chapters, my old high school's hallways were extremely tight. Part of the reason why I didn't do well there was because of the hallways.

Even though all the students' knocking into me was unintentional, it was agonizing. I felt paranoid to the point that I thought everyone wanted to reach out and grab me. I had no personal space, and I was definitely beyond my comfort zone. Frequently, I would sweat and end up with an upset stomach.

But as with my issue with sound, my comfort zone broadened as I grew older. I now don't mind people patting me on the back or giving me a hug, but I still have to have space walking in hallways and sitting at tables.

HAVE SELF-CONTROL

What has helped me a lot in controlling those sometimes-hostile impulses is maintaining self-control. Making a scene in a public place, like my incident in grade school, was inappropriate and an example of no self-control. Reacting in such a way can alienate you from other people. This can lead to bullying, loneliness, and many other unwanted consequences.

I really can't give you a list of guidelines to follow. If someone reaches out to touch me, I say something like, "I don't like to be touched, please. Is there something you need?"

With a simple courteous response, I give the other person the idea that I am aware of them, and that I am a person who doesn't like to be touched, and that the person should stop. This method may not work with every person. There maybe some occasions where a student in school might tease you and may continue to poke you. This has never happened to me, but either way, tell the person you don't like to be touched, and that they should stop. If they don't stop, then get an adult involved.

TEXTURES

From my personal experiences with Asperger's Syndrome there are various textures that I like and dislike. Since I can remember, I have had a strong attachment to soft textures. Whether it was carpet, bed sheets, pillows, or sweat pants and shirts, I could not get enough of the softness.

This wanting of softness dominated me so much that I was picky about what I wore. Through my early childhood years, I wore sweatpants and sweatshirts. Whenever my parents showed me a pair of jeans, a nice pair of trousers, or a buttoned shirt, I would refuse to wear them. I didn't find them to be that cozy compared to sweats. The other thing I didn't have an interest in wearing was woolen sweaters. They were constantly irritating and itchy. I always had the urge to tear them off my body, for they have the itchiness of a thousand mosquito bites.

It took me until I was twelve to wear something other than sweats when my parents introduced me to Cargo sports pants and slacks. Since then, I have broadened my interest in different clothes. I now wear jeans and scratchy sweaters, but I still prefer any other form of clothing to a pair of jeans.

When I was five, the one texture that I absolutely did not like was grass. The first time I walked in my family's yard barefoot, I instantly jumped away from it and ran to my mother's lap. When I touched the grass, I felt that I was touching razor sharp blades. For years, I would not walk on grass or even touch it with my hands.

At the age of ten, I decided to try to walk on grass barefoot again. When I placed my bare feet in our yard, I then realized that it wasn't as bad as I thought it was. I had outgrown my childish fear.

There is no solid advice I can give you on how to deal with sensitivity to touch. As with hearing, I have matured out of a lot of my sensitivity to touch. You may or may not mature out of such sensitivities, depending on how severe your AS condition is. It varies with each individual. But from what I have read and researched, most people who have AS outgrow such sensory sensitivities.

Note to Parents: *Enduring Pain*

Some people assume that, since people with AS are sensitive to touch, they are also sensitive to pain. It would be a false statement to say that people with AS are less tolerant of pain.

As I mentioned in the section above, whenever I walked on grass when I was little, I felt like I was walking on glass. My next-door neighbor always walked on the grass barefoot, and it never bothered him. In another instance, I fell on my knee on a concrete curb.

"Jeff, are you all right?" my mom asked.

I looked down at my knee and saw that I had made myself a bloody gash. I only shrugged. I had not felt a thing. One person may react differently to one form of pain than another. There is no way to determine who can endure what.

However, I found an interesting article on the Internet called "Asperger's Syndrome and Unequal Reaction to Pain" that explains a scientific study on why a person with Asperger's Syndrome may react differently to pain.[1] I'm not going to try to explain the study, because I am no scientist. But the web link appears in the References in the back of this book, if you are interested.

In any case, people with AS are sensitive people, whether it is to noise, sight, or even touch. I have outgrown many of my sensitivities over the years, but I still don't like loud noises or being touched without my permission.

Chapter 5

Motor Skills and Awkwardness

When my mom first mentioned *motor skills,* I asked her, "What are motor skills? Do motor skills give me the ability to fix a motor engine?"

She laughed and said, "No."

She explained to me that motor skills are related to the muscles of the body that help coordinate particular parts of it, such as the joints, feet, and hands. These skills help make the body work properly. Most people usually develop these skills in their early childhood. Many people with AS have very poor motor skills.

Throughout my grade school years, I had a funny walk, an odd way of holding a pencil, and was incapable of playing sports. In gym class, I did not have a quick reaction speed in catching a ball. My chance of catching a ball and not dropping it was one out of a hundred. I was often teased in gym class because of this.

How well you develop motor skills depends on how well you coordinate your body. There are two types of these skills: fine motor skills and gross motor skills.

FINE MOTOR SKILLS

Fine motor skills (FMS) include abilities with the hands, like manipulating small objects with your fingers or moving things from hand to hand. FMS also includes hand-eye coordination.[1] When it comes to Fine Motor Skills, my hands and fingers operate a little awkwardly compared to a normal person's. The best example I can use to illustrate this is how I hold a pencil.

An ordinary person holds a pencil by grasping it by the tube part with the index finger on one side and the thumb on the other, while the middle finger rests below the thumb and index finger. I hold a pencil by placing my index, middle, and ring fingers on one side of the pencil, while my thumb grasps the other side of it.

My parents struggled a long time to make me hold a pencil correctly, as did my kindergarten and elementary teachers. My parents even called in a physical therapist to try to help me hold a pencil correctly. But none prevailed. I never thought that there was a right or wrong way to hold a pencil. In my mind, if you can hold one and write with it without any trouble, that ought to pass.

But since I hold a pencil *differently,* I have a challenge when it comes to drawing and working with other utensils by hand. In the tenth grade, I was in Wood Shop. For the first forty days straight, there was nothing but drawing shape after shape with compasses, rulers, and a lead pencil.

It was aggravating and rather embarrassing to go to this class, because it took me several class periods to finish just one drawing.

I usually went through two or three sheets of paper before I would even get it done due to all the eraser-marks and mess-ups I had made on the previous ones. I tried to make it perfect, but I never got an A. Everyone else seemed to do drawings easily, because they finished them quicker than I did, and always got higher grades. The way I hold a pencil could very well be the reason I don't do well with drawing, but there's more to FMS than working with utensils.

For a long time, I had a major difficulty tying my shoes. Whenever they came untied, I had to have someone tie them for me. My parents tried to explain the various steps it took to tie them, but I couldn't understand all the motions it took.

I felt mortified whenever my shoes got untied in school because I always had to ask the teacher to tie them for me. It was humiliating. To conceal this embarrassment I wore Velcro shoes. It took me till my ninth birthday to finally understand the steps it took to tie my shoes. My family had to celebrate, for I finally knew how to tie my shoes!

I've acknowledged in an earlier chapter that I didn't like wearing jeans and shirts with buttons, but I loved wearing sweatshirts and pants. Not only did I like the cozy textures, but also, sweats were easy to get in and out of. Rather than having to unbutton my shirt or remove my jeans belt, I could just slide in and out of them.

Trying to get into a pair of jeans was like trying to solve a jigsaw puzzle. As with tying shoes, I didn't understand all the motions and steps it took to button jeans and pull the zipper up. In addition, I never really liked wearing a belt around my waistline because I felt that my stomach was being compressed and interfering with my ability to breathe.

VIDEO GAMES

On my tenth birthday, I got a Nintendo 64 game system. Since then, video games have become one of my main free-time hobbies. Those of you who are video game players might be wondering how video games are related to Fine Motor Skills. Well, most video games require the use of a controller to play the game. While using a controller, you're also focusing on a television or computer screen. This develops great hand-eye coordination, which is needed for other tasks in life, like typing on a computer.

When I first started typing on a computer, I would stare at the keyboard and only punch in one letter at a time. After I had punched in a letter, I would look back up at the screen to see what I had typed. After that, I would type another letter, stop, look back up at the screen, and do this again and again, until I finished whatever I was typing on the computer. At such a pace, this often took quite a while.

With my N64, the one game I was absolutely addicted to was *Zelda: Ocarina of Time*. Every quest I played as the legendary warrior, Link, involved more mental power.

I admit that when I started to play that game, it was no easy mission. It took me weeks of constant brick walls of frustration, because each level became more challenging, and the bosses were harder to take down than the ones before. But as I continued to learn how to work my controller and play the game, I gained more skill with hand-eye coordination.

After a year of gaming, I developed the ability to type with most of my fingers on a keyboard, and I was able look at the screen while I typed. I also built up many other mental skills from video gaming such as:

- Focus
- Multi-tasking
- Abstract thinking
- Problem-solving
- Perseverance
- Memory
- Quick thinking
- Reasonable judgment[2]

All of the skills listed above can apply to taking a test. You need to know and remember how to answer the questions for a test from your notes and study guide. You need reasonable judgment to decide how to answer a question when you're not sure of the answer. In some subject tests like math, you need to know abstract thinking and step-by-step problem solving.

Now, I'm not saying that video games are a study guide for tests, but from playing them, you can gain such skills as listed above. All you have to do is apply them to school and, later on, a job. But there are some negative aspects to playing video games.

Back when I got my Xbox several years ago, I received the game *Halo*. Like millions of other XBOX players, I think *Halo* is the best first person shooter video game, but after playing only this game for a very long time, I became worn out from it. I fell into a rut.

As bored as I was with it, I could not give it up. I played it over and over again. I felt like a crack-head who needed a fix every hour. In my case, I needed to play *Halo* every hour.

So why didn't I just turn the game console off and walk away? Like all other video games, *Halo* contains a new threat or a challenge that keeps you motivated to play the game. I was relieved when I reached a new checkpoint, but I also had an urge to go on.

I grew addicted to *Halo*. I played only *Halo* for a full year before I moved on to other games. Video games can be very addictive. It may seem cool to play the same game, but after a while it can grow into an obsession. I read in an article that about nine out of ten kids in the U.S. play video games at least an hour a day. And sixty-four percent of video game players spend at least two or more hours a day playing them.[3] That's quite time-consuming, since there are only twenty-four hours in a day!

Reading such statistics on video game players made me realize not only how much time I was spending on video games, but also how much time I was losing on other things I could be doing with my life. I decided to quit playing *Halo* for a while, and move on to other games and activities such as reading and writing. When I finished writing a fun short story or reading a book, I felt I had accomplished something more than just shooting monsters on a screen.

It has been a long time since I last played *Halo*. I still enjoy the game, but it's not as much an addiction as it once was. Instead of playing a video game for four to six hours a day, I limit myself to gaming one or two hours a day, and I only play on weekends. The rest of the week, I devote myself to other things that I find more valuable.

For you video game players, try to find other activities that interest you besides video games. Now I'm not saying video games are a bad thing, just don't make it an obsession or a dominating factor in your life. If you are a gamer, try to enjoy playing a variety of games. The games I like to play more of nowadays are the ones that involve a lot of thinking, like *Rome: Total War*. Not only does it make my gaming time go by faster, but I also find it more satisfying.

I still enjoy wreaking havoc upon a bunch of harmful creatures that keep charging at me by the hundreds, but I find that it gets tiresome after a while, since it is the same thing over and over again, just at a different level. Any video game you play, have fun with it.

For those of you aren't video game players, its okay that you don't play them. There are many other activities out there that involve hand-eye coordination such as dancing, baseball, basketball, and playing an instrument.[4] Get out and do something you enjoy.

GROSS MOTOR SKILLS

Since I first started to walk, I trotted like a penguin. My feet stuck outwards like a "V" rather than being aligned, and I wobbled to each side as I made my strides. My parents kept telling me to keep my feet together in a straight line. I did try, but my feet wouldn't cooperate. I always felt that my feet had a mind of their own, but this of course was not the answer to the mystery. I lacked proper Gross Motor Skills.

Gross Motor Skills (GMS) are related to the larger muscles throughout the body that help with tasks like lifting your head up, sitting up, crawling, and walking. These motor skills develop action and good coordination, as well as posture, perceptual skills, and balance.[5]

When I was toddler, I had a bad experience of tripping down the stairs. For several years after that incident, I had the fear of falling down a flight of stairs. I always wanted to make sure I had my feet on the correct step. Instead of touching each stair with one foot and placing the other on the next step, I would put my other foot on the same step and halt for a second before proceeding to the next step. It probably took me a couple of minutes to walk up or down the fifteen steps in my house.

My mom calls this being earthbound. I liked to make sure my feet were always on the ground. But when I did this, I had a habit of not being mindful of my surroundings. My parents frequently had to stop me from colliding with other people when I walked with my head bowed.

This changed, though, when my family and I went on vacation to Niagara Falls. On one of the days we were there, we went to a restaurant that had revolving doors. It was not a big deal entering them, since no one else was in them. So I took my time going through them.

On our way out, though, there was a man behind us who seemed to be in a bit of a hurry. He cut in front of me and pushed through the revolving doors quickly. After he had passed through them, I then entered the revolving doors, not paying any attention to how fast the revolving doors were spinning. Suddenly, my dad grabbed my hand and pulled me out of the revolving door.

"Dang it Jeff, how many times do I have to tell you to always look up?!" he growled.

"What, what's wrong?" I asked, dazed.

"You almost got your arm stuck in that door!" he bellowed.

After that little incident in Niagara Falls, I became more mindful of my surroundings. Without being knowledgeable about your surroundings, you never know who or what you could run into.

FLEXIBILITY

Lacking Gross Motor Skills can also affect your flexibility. You may be flexible in some parts of your body but inflexible with others. My arms and my legs have always been flexible. According to my doctor, I can expand my arm joints to a hundred-and-ninety-two degree incline. I can also put my foot behind my head.

A few years ago, I had yoga sessions with a physical therapist. There I learned a lot about my flexibility as well as my inflexibility. There are certain positions I have no trouble with. I can position my legs outwards like a "V" and slide my body all the way to the ground without hurting myself.

However, there are the other positions I can't do. One yoga position my physical therapist taught me was called the frog. It involved squatting, feet flat on the ground, and pulling your body close to the floor. I could squat to the floor fine, but I could not keep my feet flat on the ground or keep my balance. I could only do it with my tiptoes touching the floor.

I don't want you to think that you're flexible or inflexible because of having AS. Many people who have AS are inflexible. But many people who don't have AS are inflexible too. My dad doesn't have AS, and he's not that flexible. Nonetheless, inflexibility and lack of motor skills are common characteristics of persons with AS.

CLUMSINESS, WHAT TO DO ABOUT IT?

People who lack proper Gross Motor Skills can be clumsy. My clumsiness was most obvious in the way I ate. I would repeatedly chew with my mouth open, which often led food falling out of my mouth and landing on my lap. In addition, I always hunched over the table when I ate, which led to more food landing on my shirt.

When it came to foods that involved utensils, I would use them in very peculiar ways. With pasta, instead of twirling it with my fork, I would cut the noodles up into pieces and then shove each bit in my mouth. When some of the noodles would begin to fall off of my fork,

I would quickly suck them up like a bird with a worm. Disgusting, I know, but that's how I ate.

This changed in the tenth grade when I went on a field trip to a fancy place called The Oasis. There I learned to act more like a gentleman instead of a slob when it comes to the dinner table. I learned from this place that eating food with utensils has rules and that I had to obey and use them properly. I originally had the theory that as long my body felt nourished I was doing well. That is not necessarily the case, though.

It came to me that if I wanted to eat out in public, I had to give some thought to modifying my behavior. There have to be manners while eating at a table, especially in a public place. I have to be neat with my utensils, place a napkin on my lap, wear a bib, if necessary, and sit up in my seat rather than hunch over, to avoid making a mess on my shirt.

Since that trip to The Oasis, rarely does food end up on my shirt or lap. I still have my occasional messes, but I don't have to throw my shirt in the laundry every day. There's not much I can tell you about any problems you may have with motor skills and clumsiness. I know many people without AS who are clumsy. But if your motor skills are quite "off key," it may be wise to have a physical therapist help you out.

As I've mentioned earlier, I had a physical therapist. For several years, she helped me greatly with my balance, walking patterns, and some of my other bodily quirks. To this day though, I still hold a pencil differently than most people do.

Chapter 6

Stress & Its Associates

I can tell you from experience that stress is my number-one enemy. It is an overwhelming flood that can be absolutely controlling, as if a foreign dictator ran my mind. It makes me tense and on edge every second.

From my past encounters with stress, I have also discovered that it can branch off into varying dramatic feelings and emotions including anxiety, anger, and meltdowns. I have come to call these emotions "stress associates." They are soon to follow when stress arrives. Stress can also bring on depression, which makes things even more unpleasant.

I don't want you to get the wrong impression of stress; it is not a villain. Everyone encounters stress daily, and it can be managed.

MELTDOWNS AND ANXIETY

Back in the eighth grade, I had an unexpected pop quiz. My IEP prohibits me from taking pop quizzes, but I got one from my math teacher. She either did not pay attention to the IEP, or forgot what it said about pop quizzes.

I suddenly had a twenty-point test that I had been unaware of, and I freaked out. After the stress kicked in, I began feeling anxious. Following my anxiety, I got depressed because I was afraid that I would get a bad grade, which would damage my grade point average. When the depression gripped me, my mind had a meltdown. Through the whole class, I sat at my desk, staring blankly at the quiz.

When the bell finally rang, I started to leave for my next class, but my teacher stopped me.

She asked, "Jeff, where is your test?"

"I didn't do it," I replied.

"What?"

"I didn't do it because I didn't feel prepared for it," I answered. That day did not go well for either of us. I had to take the quiz the following day, and my teacher had to have a talk with my mom about me not having pop quizzes.

Stress can create a chain of emotions. I have passed from one state of emotion to another. There are times that I just get anxious or mad. But under more dire circumstances, like having to take a sudden quiz, my mind just goes blank.

I have done some very idiotic things in the past when I was stressed, like my walking out of school in the ninth grade. I have to get away from a stressful environment to cool down, or I'd go nuts. I usually did this without the staff's consent.

Other times, I would get so overloaded with stress, as I had with that pop quiz, that I would mentally block out everything around me. If someone talked to me, I would not respond. A person would have to poke me in order to rouse me from such a state. It has always been difficult for me to control the urge to do something rash because of stress and its associates.

FIND THE SOURCE

During the times I'm anxious, people often tell me to "Chill out," "Relax." Just chilling doesn't cut it. There is no simple way to automatically get rid of stress. But there are different ways to cope with it.

The key to dealing with stress is to identify the cause of it. The pop quiz I had to take triggered my anxiety. There was no way to avoid taking the test. Even though it was a pop quiz, it was still an assignment that had to be completed. I knew the material, but my anxiety blinded me. Delaying it by a day gave me a chance to relax and get some studying done so I could be better prepared. Once you find the source of what's creating your stress, whether it's a test or anything else, you can find ways of coping with it.

YOGA

I mentioned in the previous chapter that I took yoga lessons with a physical therapist. Not only does yoga help stretch and coordinate my body better, but it also helps me cope under stressful situations.

When I was thirteen, my parents decided to take me up to Cedar

Point so I could ride on the roller coaster, "the Millennium Force." I was thrilled to death, but I felt a bit nervous. Nevertheless, I was confident that I would ride the Millennium force. After a six-hour drive, we finally arrived.

As soon as I laid my eyes on that monster of a roller coaster, my jaw dropped to the ground. I had never seen such a colossal roller coaster in my whole life. The starting hill seemed to reach the heavens and the screams of the people on the ride were barely audible.

All kinds of crazy thoughts entered my mind as I saw this colossal sight. *Are the seat guards and belts going to hold me in the coaster? Am I going to fall off that hill? Is the coaster going to break off the tracks?* Needless to say, I did not want to go on the ride, but my dad convinced me to get in the line that appeared to go on for miles.

Every step closer we took in the line, I begged my dad, "Do we have to go on it? We don't have to do it if you don't want to."

My dad laughed at me and persuaded me to stay in line and that I would be all right. When we finally reached the coaster, I froze. My anxiety was going through the roof.

"What are you waiting for?" my dad asked as he was about to climb in the coaster.

"I can't do this," I told him.

"Oh, yes, you can," he said.

"No, I can't," I pleaded.

"We waited for an hour in this line, and you're not quitting on me now!"

Sweat was beading down my head and my heart was racing. But then I reminded myself of the deep breathing techniques my yoga therapist had taught me. I took a few deep breaths and quickly stretched my back.

"Jeff, you can do this," I told myself. I climbed into the coaster and tightened myself with the seatbelt and the overhead restraint bar. The next three minutes were among the most thrilling in my life.

"You need to identify the bad, but focus on the good," my dad told me after we got off the roller coaster. "Focusing on the bad will get you nowhere, but focusing on the good gets you somewhere."

If I had chickened out, I would have missed the best roller coaster ride ever. I even told my dad after the ride that I wanted to go on it again. Unfortunately, the line was way too long, and it was getting close to dinnertime.

With the combination of a few deep breaths and some positive thinking, I made myself ride the biggest and best ride ever. Whether you're going on a huge roller coaster or even taking a test, take a few deep breaths and tell yourself that you can do it.

EXPRESS YOURSELF

Whenever I was bullied, I always kept my emotions and stress bottled up. I wouldn't tell my parents about it until a week or even a month after a bullying incident had occurred.

My mom said to me on many occasions, "Jeff, you need to be open with your feelings. If you don't tell me what's bothering you now, I can't help you. You can't be a clam all your life."

As an individual with Asperger's Syndrome, it is hard for me to express my emotions or even to tell my parents if something is bugging me. A lot of times, I was embarrassed, because I didn't want to be seen in school as a person who tattletales.

Now that I am older, I can better express myself when things are vexing me. There are still times when I am bottled up like a clam, but talking to someone about my troubles has been good medicine for relieving my stress.

BE INVOLVED SPIRITUALLY

I was never much of a church-going person. But when I started Bible studies with my grandfather, my stress decreased. In addition, I gained some religious faith.

Of the books I have read in the Bible, the one that really caught my interest the most was Job. I could relate to him a lot. Job was a man who was happy, proud, and great, but then lost everything. Despite the cruel things that happen to him, he remains faithful to God, which ultimately saves him. I know what it is like to feel miserable and without hope.

Since I gained an interest in reading the Bible, I feel that I'm a better person than I was. I'm not trying to preach, but if you pursue a religion or a certain deity, gaining some faith in it can make you feel better and give you some hope during rough times. My grandfather once told me that a little bit of faith can go a long way.

MUSIC

Ever since I can remember, I have loved listening to music. Whether it is upbeat rock' n 'roll or classical music, it brings a joy that rescues me from every stressful situation. Since I have such a passion for music, my parents bought me an I-POD in my junior year of high school. Now I can bring and listen to my music whenever I want to. I-PODs can be expensive though, and depending on your school's rules, you may or may not be allowed to bring any electronic devices into the building.

With the teachers' and school's approval, you should be able to bring your music with you. This doesn't give you the privilege to listen to it in class during the teachers' lectures. Listen to your music only in your free time, such as at lunch or between classes. But be careful with your I-POD, because other kids can be scavengers.

I once lost a pair of headphones because I wasn't keeping a sharp eye on them. I went almost an entire week without listening to my I-POD because I couldn't find my earphones. As a consequence, I had to buy a new pair, which cost over thirty dollars. Always be careful with your belongings.

Note to Parents: *Have a Plan B*

There'll be times when your AS child will get stressed. It is best to be prepared in case he has a meltdown or an anxiety attack at school. Now I'm not saying that your AS child has a stress and anxiety disorder, but it is very common for someone with AS to develop such a disorder as well as have difficulty expressing various emotions such as anger, sadness, and even fear.

From junior high on, my mom has arranged a series of plans with my interventionalists and guidance counselors for there to be places I could go whenever I get stressed or have a meltdown. If I was ever having any trouble, I was allowed to leave class and go to the IEP room, so I could cool off and get my work done in a calmer environment. When my mom and the school established this plan as an accommodation, I knew I had a "safe spot" to go to when I was stressed out.

It would be wise for your AS kid to have a place or two to head to when she is overwhelmed and can't concentrate in class, whether it is an interventionalist's room or a guidance counselor's office, as long as it's somewhere your AS child can relax and recuperate.

PHYSICAL EFFECTS

Stress and its associates can affect you physically as much as mentally and emotionally. Did you know that stress is a leading cause of death? Having a great load of stress, anxiety, anger, or depression can lead to suicide, a variety of cancers, and heart failure.[1]

There are other symptoms that stress and its associates can bring on, such as fatigue, headaches, aches and pains, lack of appetite, and sleep problems.[2] A few summers ago, I felt constipation and indigestion after I ate. I did not know why I had these aches and pains in my abdomen.

An agonizing week later, I saw my doctor. There I learned that I had

Irritable Bowel Syndrome (IBS). IBS is when a person's digestive system is sensitive and becomes agitated very easily. Too much stress can affect your internal organs. Stress attacks my stomach. Whenever I feel stress building up, I feel my stomach churning and boiling.

In the sixth grade, I had difficulty getting to sleep. Some nights I became restless, and would get little or no sleep. I would toss and turn, trying to get in a comfy position as my thoughts wandered aimlessly over what had to be accomplished the next day. Usually, by the time I fell unconscious, it was almost time to get up for the next day. From my experience, there are a number of reasons for being unable to snooze.

- sleeping disorders
- side-effects of medications
- aches and pains
- night cramps

I was fortunate that this issue did not go on for too long; I was introduced to new medications that knocked me out like a log. There may be several causes of insomnia; nonetheless, if you have sleeping issues like I had, it is best you tell someone about it, whether it is your parents or your doctor. There are a few additional tips that I have come up with that may be useful for helping you get a better night's sleep.

- Read a book or an article before going to sleep.
- Get yourself in a comfortable position in your bed.

- Exercise
- Listen to some calm music.

Block out all the lights and pull down the blinds in your room to make it dark.

Do everything that needs to be done and ready for the next day. This way, you'll be more prepared for the next morning, and you won't have to worry whether you forgot to put something in your backpack or not.

Don't eat or snack too late. One time, as I was staying up for New Year's Eve, I had a bit of candy and cake. When the ball dropped on for the New Year, I went to bed, thinking I would get a good night's sleep for the start of the New Year. Shortly after falling asleep, I woke up with horrible abdominal pain. I was stuck on the pot for thirty minutes. Trying to get back to bed after such an experience isn't that easy.

It takes several hours for the stomach to digest food and, with an active stomach, it's difficult to get a decent night's sleep. That's why I now never eat past seven on school nights or past eight on weekends. I'm not saying that you're guaranteed to have trouble if you eat late, but I wouldn't take the chance. For me there's nothing worse than not getting a good night's sleep.

ANGER MANAGEMENT

In the later junior high to early high school years, I had problems expressing my anger. When I flew into a tantrum at school, I was inclined to punch walls and lockers. I was fortunate to not cause any damage to the school or myself. There are many things that can set me off, including someone cutting me off on the interstate while I'm driving, or someone poking fun at me. When I'm angry, I release my anger in two different ways: explosively or implosively.

An example of being explosive with anger was in my tenth-grade science class. In the middle of the second semester, I had to take a hundred-point test. I had studied vigorously the previous night, and I felt I understood the material. I took the test, and I felt confident that I had gotten a decent grade on it. When I got the test back, I learned that I had flunked it. I was outraged by this result.

Without a thought, I charged out of the classroom into the hallway and began randomly punching and kicking lockers while cursing. When I punched the lockers, I released much of my rage by taking it out on them. I was no longer upset after I had pummeled them, but my knuckles were sore for a week.

Someone with explosive anger usually releases it from their system as soon as it begins to bug them. If you explode every time something goes wrong, you're letting your anger control you, and you do rash things. As bad as explosive anger can be, a person with this type of anger at least gets it out of his system quickly.

With implosive anger, a person allows things to bother them, giving it time to build up to the point of fracture. There was a specific day back in the sixth grade where everything seemed to go wrong. I was late in getting up in the morning, the cafeteria had no food that I wanted to eat, and after the bad lunch I realized that I had forgotten to bring a hefty point project for my science class.

I decided that I had enough. Instead of going to my science class to tell my teacher that I had forgotten my project, I bolted towards the parking lot at the front entrance and began shrieking at the top of my lungs. The principal found me outside when he looked out his window. After he brought me inside, he called my mom to help calm me down.

Neither type of anger is healthy. Letting anger boil inside of you isn't good. Getting angry over every little thing isn't wise either. I knew a kid back in the seventh grade who fell into a frenzy over the littlest things, whether a person asked him a question or if he dropped his books. Because of his violent outbursts, he alienated himself from everyone as a lunatic rather than being someone with whom people would want to be friends. Like many other students, I was afraid to be around him, because I didn't know when he might suddenly explode.

That's an impression you don't want to give other people. I'm not saying you have to smile through your anger or be happy all the time. It is normal to get angry, but blowing up in a public place and doing rash things like shouting, cursing, punching, or throwing things, is inappropriate. Violence is not the way to go in unleashing your anger.

When I ran out of the school into the parking lot, I was not controlling my anger. I was unleashing it. I've learned from my experiences of ballistic outbursts to reveal my exasperation only where I won't draw attention to myself or get into trouble. There is no denying that it is hard to manage, but there are ways of putting out the raging fire of anger.

TIPS ON MANAGING ANGER

If you feel the urge to hit something, I suggest punching a pillow. Hitting a pillow is safer and better than hitting metal lockers and concrete walls. There are other times I am so infuriated that I just have to scream at the top of my lungs. When I have this urge, I wait until I get home from school, walk out onto the deck outside, and let it all out.

Yelling and punching pillows have helped me a lot when I was really ticked off over something. This doesn't mean that it'll work for you, though. Screaming and punching things could provoke your anger rather than tame it. I have to admit that there are times I get a little carried away with my anger; sometimes it can't wait until I get home.

Anger is like an unpredictable bomb. It can go off either when it reaches its mark, or just go off unexpectedly. That's why I often walk away from whatever is aggravating me.

One time I was working on a very challenging movie project for my Digital Design class. I had to edit the film on a computer at school and make it as perfect as I could. The darn PC kept having system failures and it wouldn't load or save the work I had done the days prior. I wanted to grab the computer and throw it across the classroom.

If I had done that, I probably would have been expelled. Instead of continuing to work on the computer with my vexation building, I strolled away from it and asked permission from my teacher to go and talk to the guidance counselor about my intense feelings.

It is best to just walk away from the issue rather than charge through it like a bull. If you feel this way in class, I suggest that you ask your teacher if you can take a break from it. This was another reason my mom had those "safe spots" set up for me.

Talking to someone, whether it's to my family, close friends, or my therapist, has helped me a lot in dealing with my anger. Even if I was just ranting and raving the whole time, I always felt better when someone listened to me. Never be afraid to ask a teacher, your parents, or a guidance counselor to sit down and talk with you about your feelings.

Another thing that has helped when I get angry is writing my feelings down on a piece of scrap paper. Afterwards I crumple up the paper and toss it away. When I write my feelings down, I feel that I have expressed myself and am able to move on. Give it a shot. Expressing emotions through written words can be therapeutic.

Now, these are tips on how to manage anger. They may not necessarily reduce your anger when it comes, but many of the tips that have helped reduce my stress have also helped to decrease my anger. They may work for you, too.

It is quite a normal thing to get angry at times, but don't go ballistic over everything that vexes you. Everyone has their breaking point. Don't let it get the best of you.

DEPRESSION

Stress can also lead to depression. It can create hormonal shifts in the brain, which in turn can cause mood swings and changes.[3] There are other things that can contribute to depression, such as:

- a poor diet
- certain medications
- exposure to toxic metals
- a death in the family
- a hereditary gene[4]

When I was twelve, my father got very ill. Before this unfortunate event, I was a giddy little kid who was not easily disheartened. But when I learned about his illness, my happiness vanished, and I was sucked into a foggy atmosphere of depression.

Asperger's Syndrome kicked in, and I obsessed over his condition. Things did get a little better when his health improved, but then two other things worsened my depression. They were the terrorist attacks on the World Trade Center and puberty. The horrible images on television of the collapse of the two towers filled my mind with depressing thoughts. I kept having nightmares of being trapped in a burning building.

Following the onset of puberty, my mood kept changing on me like the hills and dips in a roller coaster. I would be elated one minute and sullen the next. I also started growing body and facial hair and developed unforgiving acne.

On and off for three years, I wandered in the gloomy mist of depression. I felt hopeless and worthless. I couldn't concentrate in school very well, and I could not find much pleasure in anything. I had restless nights of sleep, and I even developed some recurring aches and pains in my back, legs, and abdomen.

From the articles I have read on depression, I learned that there are many different types. I could go on and list them, but that would be getting away from the intention of the book. It is hard to diagnose someone with depression due to the number of symptoms and the different types of it. Before you jump to conclusions as to whether you have depression, it is best to gain the counsel of a doctor. It can be treated therapeutically and with proper medications.

Pills can be helpful, but they don't create miracles. As I've said before, they can actually be quite dangerous, and some medications can make matters worse. I was put on a drug back in the eighth grade called Wellbutrin™. Instead of the medication making me feel better, it made matters worse for me.

I started having paranoid thoughts. I feared that all my peers at school were saying bad things about me behind my back. This also was the time in my life when I had issues about my appearance and scary thoughts of being different from everyone else because of my AS.

It became so horrible that I had to withdraw from school for weeks at a time. I was then put on a "trial and error." This is a method that doctors use to figure out which drugs are helpful for their patients, and which ones are not. It took roughly three years before the medications worked. A trial and error regimen can take a few months to a few years.

Medication should always be a last resort. But if your doctor suggests that you go on a medication, you should at least consider it as an option. It is always a good idea for you and your parents to research it on your own so you know what to expect. Often, a quick Google search will provide lists of possible side effects and sometimes even testimonials from people who have taken that particular drug. Keep in mind that the information will be biased, based on people's personal experiences and chemical makeups, but it is still information you can consider before you start taking a new drug. Make sure you consult with your doctor about dosage and side effects before you start taking it, as well as any other questions or concerns you may have. Perhaps you could start off with a half dose to see if that does the trick. But do not alter the dosage on your own. It's important that you take the prescription as prescribed so the doctor can properly assess and monitor the results. If you are ever concerned about how a medication is affecting you, whether you've just started taking it or you've been taking it for a while, tell your doctor immediately.

With the combination of proper medication and talk therapy, I have risen out of my depressive rut. There are still times though when I am down "in the blues" for various reasons.

Sometimes it takes more than pills and therapy to fight depression. During my troubles, I read a book called *Questions Young People Ask*. It's a bit on the religious side, but every time I read it, it opens my eyes to my problems. At the end of each chapter, the book has questions related to the chapter and the questions are answerable. Of all the questions I read in the book's chapters, there were two that really stood out.

"Is it up to others to measure your worth as a person? ... are (you) depressed over some weakness or sin you have committed?"[5]

Is it up to others to measure my worth as person? For many years, I did what I could to be accepted and well-liked in school. In late junior high to early high school, I made weird noises and did impersonations of certain popular movie characters such as Master Yoda and Gollum.

I seemed to get popular for a while since every person I encountered in the hallway asked me to say, "My Precious, Gollum, Gollum." Right after I would make an impersonation, I would try to ask them a question, but before I could, they would walk away. I soon learned that everyone was interested only in the weird voices I could make rather than what I was really like. I then realized that I could not spend the rest of my life trying to please everyone. I am me.

However, there are some exceptions. During one of my summer breaks, I decided to get myself a job. To get the job, I had to make a good impression on the person I was meeting. I dressed in nice clothes, took care of my personal hygiene and put on my best attitude. I didn't get it, since the job required experience in a field that was outside my knowledge, but the man told me it had been a pleasure to meet me.

Even though I'm not obsessed with how I appear to others, I do try to show other people that I'm an easy person to get along with and not a troublemaker. Most people seem to like me at school and at church, but I am not perfect. There are days I am angry, and I might say something that someone may find offensive. There may even be some people who just don't like me at all.

Am I depressed over some weakness or sin I may have committed? No. My dad's illness is beyond my control. I can't blame myself for him being ill. Nor did I contribute to having trouble with puberty. Everyone goes through puberty. It is unavoidable, and it affects everyone differently.

After I had reflected on and answered these questions, I felt I had solved my puzzle. When I finished reading the book, I felt more relieved about my inner turmoil with depression.

BE WISE ABOUT YOUR ENTERTAINMENT

There are shows, music, and movies out there that can make you feel gloomy and depressed. I don't find it smart to watch or listen to something that has a dismal atmosphere, such as *The Untouchables*. One of the characters I liked in that movie meets a brutal death, which disturbed me. Entertainment that contains such explicit violence can promote aggressive and sullen thoughts.

Whenever I feel down I watch a classic satire like *Monty Python: the Holy Grail*. Every time I see that movie, I laugh as hard as if I had seen it for the first time. I find that laughing is a good therapy that helps distract me from my problems. However, there have been times when, after watching a funny movie, I start feeling sad again the very next day or even the next hour.

I usually watch comedies, but I don't like seeing movies of the same genre over and over again. So sometimes, in order to get rid of my gloominess, I have to listen to a song or watch a movie that is depressing.

I know this sounds like a contradiction, but when I watch the film *Schindler's List*, I am saddened by the graphic depiction of the Holocaust, and I cry each time I watch it. As saddening as that movie is, I feel better after seeing it because it lets my sorrow out.

I don't want give you mixed messages on how to entertain yourself, for it is up to you. When I need to watch something funny, I put in a comedy. If I need to cry, I watch a tearjerker. Both genres, though dissimilar, help me out in my times of depression. It just depends on what I'm up for.

DON'T HANG AROUND INDIVIDUALS WHO ARE A BAD INFLUENCE

In the eighth grade, I hung around with disrespectful individuals who cursed teachers behind their backs and called kids who were popular in school "preps." I know school society is difficult and, for a long time, I wanted to blend in with my peers. I tried hanging out with different groups and individuals to see if I could find my niche.

I felt most comfortable around the Goths and skinheads, because I felt they understood the pain and aggression that was caused by puberty, the school society's attitude towards me, and my father's illness. But I only felt worse when I hung around those individuals. Having such a harsh attitude towards everyone fed my paranoia and depression.

When I'm depressed, I have a tendency to fixate on the reasons why I am so dispirited. I only became more vexed when I thought like this. There is nothing more depressing than being angry with yourself for being depressed.

My dad has always told me to look at the good in every situation, even if it appears hopeless. Being optimistic can help you out of the gloom. Elation is more uplifting than being a grump. That's why I don't hang out with persons who are a bad influence.

DO SOMETHING YOU ENJOY; SET REALISTIC GOALS

Anytime I have the blues, I do the things I enjoy, and I set a realistic goal regarding those hobbies. I know I am not capable of joining the varsity basketball team, but I am capable of writing a novel-length story. In my tenth-grade creative writing class, I was given a week-long assignment to write a rough draft for a short story. I had wanted to write a fantasy for a long time. On the first night I was given the assignment, I typed like I never had before. In the first two days, I had written a five-page chapter.

My creative writing teacher was so amazed by my writing that she wanted me to continue to write it. So I set myself a goal to write a rough draft of the full story. After I had set myself that goal, I made my path towards it. Through my sophomore and into my junior year, I had completed over a three-hundred-page draft. I feel great when I do something I enjoy. Writing that first draft also made me feel that I had accomplished something.

Do the things you enjoy. Set realistic goals that you are capable of accomplishing. Do whatever you can to fight depression. It is your mind. If you are interested in learning more about depression, you can check out the References at the back of the book.

A POSITIVE VIEW

As odd as it may sound, stress can actually be a good thing. Stress can make me go nuts, but it is also something that I need. Stress keeps me motivated and reminds me to get things done. Whenever I have an upcoming test for school, I feel stressed. But it reminds me to study the night before the test so I can be prepared and do well on it. If you control your stress, you can use it to meet your needs, fulfill your duties, and to accomplish your goals.

Stress also gives me an adrenaline rush. The weights I lift at the gym are challenging, and there are times when I can't get the twelve reps finished on each machine. But when I feel stressed, I use it to help me lift weights. By the time I've finished, I have usually lifted around twenty- to thirty thousand pounds. Stress can give you a lot of energy. In that case use it to exercise, but don't push yourself too hard, because you don't want to injure yourself.

Note to Parents: *You're the Rock*

Stress and its associates are encountered daily. They can come from many different sources and can cause several different emotions. Having to put up with them is hard, and there are times I feel I can't handle them all alone. All my life, I've relied on my parents for aid. Your Asperger's child counts on you to help with his issues. You need to be a rock for your AS child. Listen to him and help him.

There may be times when your AS child may not want to talk to you about his feelings. In that case, don't pressure him into talking; it could make matters worse. When I'm not comfortable talking to my parents, I speak either with my school's guidance counselor or my therapist. There are some things I'd rather not talk about with my parents. Your AS kid might feel he needs to do this. Respect his privacy.

Chapter 7

Oh No, Driving!

A lot of teenagers I know jump up and down and chant, "Woo-hoo! I'm gonna get my license when I turn sixteen!" Driving gives you a lot of freedom, but with it comes a huge responsibility. It is the first big step into reality.

Some teens I know have gotten speeding tickets or license suspensions; others have ended up in auto accidents, a couple of which resulted in injury and death. This is all from being careless with their responsibilities. Turning sixteen doesn't mean you automatically get a driver's license, nor is it the age you have to get one. There's much more to driving than just hitting the gas pedal and cranking up the vehicle's radio.

The only time you should start driving is when you feel ready for taking on such a task, and with your parent's approval. I didn't get my driver's license until I was seventeen because I did not feel prepared for such a responsibility earlier.

KNOW YOUR VEHICLE

Before I even thought of getting my license, I had to know all aspects of how to operate a vehicle. All cars have brakes, a gas pedal, mirrors, and countless other parts, but each one is a little different than another. Every time I drive a car that is new to me, I feel as though I'm driving a vehicle that is foreign.

The first vehicle I learned to drive was my mom's Mountaineer. It is high up from the ground, which makes it easy to see around traffic. Her Mountaineer also has a good turning radius, not many blind spots, and the knobs and buttons for the radio and air conditioner and heater are easy to access on the dashboard.

However, as an individual who is over six feet tall, it is hard for me to fit in her Mountaineer because the front seats don't go back far enough. When I drive her Mountaineer, I feel like a giant in a midget's car. Despite this problem, the Mountaineer is easy to handle.

After I started to learn how to drive my mom's vehicle, I also began learning how to drive my dad's Oldsmobile. It was quite different compared to my mom's vehicle, since it was low to the ground, which did not give me the advantage of seeing above and around traffic. The car also had a horrible turning radius and many blind spots.

In addition, there were many different knobs and buttons on the dashboard that made it hard for me to figure out which ones were for the air conditioner, heater, and stereo.

One time when I was driving with my dad, the front windshield fogged up. I looked down at the dashboard to try and locate the defroster. I didn't know what button or knob it was. I grew very anxious. Rather than diverting my attention from driving to finding the defroster, I rubbed the windshield with my hand to clear the fog away.

"Jeff, what are you doing?" my dad asked, alarmed.

"I'm wiping the fog away so I can see out the windshield," I told him.

"You know the knob is right here," he said, pointing to some knob on the dashboard.

"Well, your car has so many buttons and knobs on it that I feel like I'm driving James Bond's Aston Martin," I told him.

He laughed. "But rubbing your hand over the windshield smears it."

I was able to see through the windshield again, but the next day, my dad told me he had a little trouble seeing as he drove to work.

Cars vary. One car can be totally different from another. You need to make sure you're comfortable in any vehicle you drive, and know how to operate it before you get behind the wheel.

PLACES TO START DRIVING

I began my driving experience in the neighborhood. My mom and I drove every day or every-other day for a month, so I got a good feel for how her Mountaineer handled, as well as my dad's Oldsmobile.

In my opinion, driving around your own neighborhood is the best place to start your driving experience. Other places I'd suggest are cemeteries and empty parking lots. These three places are spacious, have little or no traffic and the speed limits are lower. Later on, when I felt I was ready to expand my driving knowledge, I branched off into driving on the town roads, following the highways and interstates.

Don't expect to be a professional driver like a millionaire's chauffeur when you start out. The first day I started driving with my mom I was nervous, and I kept reminding myself that I was moving a two-ton vehicle that was worth thousands of dollars. I drove slowly, going ten miles less than the neighborhood's speed limit.

Over time, you'll improve your abilities and become a better driver. I now have a couple of years of driving behind me, but I learn more about being behind the wheel of a car every day.

PERCEPTION

When behind the wheel of a car, you must be aware of your surroundings. When I began driving, I would look only at the road ahead rather than checking out my mirrors. One time, when I was driving on a country road with my mom, a car that I did not see behind me crossed the double yellow line and cut in front of me. It scared the bejesus out of me. Following that car, two more vehicles passed me. I looked down at my speedometer, and I saw that I was going a few miles under the speed limit.

I learned from this experience that just staring at the road ahead of me while driving does not work. You have to be aware of red lights, signs, other cars on the road, and any obstacles that may be in the way.

This was a struggle when I started driving, because, as a person with AS, I liked to focus on one thing at time. It requires a lot of multi-tasking to be a good driver. This makes driving a very difficult skill to acquire. This is when mirrors come in handy.

"The most important thing about driving is adjusting and using your mirrors," my mom told me on many occasions. "Mirrors help give you a good view of your vehicle's surroundings. It also gives you the position of your vehicle. This is especially important when parking. You don't want to nick someone's car while trying to back into a parking spot."

Staring straight ahead while driving for a period of time can also make a person develop *highway hypnosis*. My driving instructor defined this as "a state in which a person gets so exhausted from driving that they can doze off."

Highway hypnosis can affect a person very easily. On one of my driving lessons with my instructor, I drove on a highway for thirty miles. It was a flat road that had no red lights or signs. There was hardly anyone else on the road, and the only scenery was cornfields. The road seemed to go and on. After a while I felt tired. It was tempting to fall asleep, but I kept my eyes constantly moving as I drove.

I looked at the road, the few cars ahead of me, and in all of the vehicle's mirrors to see if anyone was behind me. And if need be, I turned my head around to see if the coast was clear so I could make a safe turn into another lane. Keeping your eyes constantly moving is a good technique to use while driving. Not only does it keep you awake, but it also makes you mindful of your surroundings.

VIGILANCE

When I was thirteen, my mom and I were waiting at an intersection on an interstate's ramp. As the cross street's traffic light turned red, a car ran through it. Another car, on our side of the right-hand lane, also made a go for it. My mom and I watched helplessly as the two cars collided. Luckily, no one was seriously injured.

After witnessing this accident, I realized that anything could happen on the road. Car accidents aren't anything like I've seen in movies. There's not always fire or thunderous, awe-inspiring explosions. In fact, there's nothing exciting about them. They are quite terrifying. For a second, I thought the car that went through the red light was going to smash into the front of my mom's Mountaineer. This is an example of why drivers need to be vigilant.

As a person with Asperger's Syndrome, I like things to be kept at a steady, uninterrupted flow, with no unanticipated surprises. But this is not how it works on the road. Roads don't change much, but the people on them do.

People are unpredictable. You never know when someone might pull out in front of you, cut you off, suddenly slam on their brakes, or even run a red light. According to my driving instructor, one out of three teenagers ends up in an accident in their first year of driving.

Being on the road can be dangerous. I may not have as much driving experience as my parents, but I know that some routes are more dangerous than others. I always like driving on the interstate because there are no red lights or stop signs, and the speed limits are higher.

With higher speed limits though, some drivers have a tendency to drive very fast. Where I live, the interstate speed limits are in the 55-70 miles-per-hour range. Every time I get on the interstate, I go the speed limit, and yet cars zoom past me as if I were sitting still.

I feel tense on the interstate because I never know when some crazy driver will pass my left- or right-hand side like a speeding bullet. Not all people obey the rules on the interstates and other roadways.

People also change lanes and go at different paces, which makes things disorganized. But there have been times I've driven on the interstate when there are hardly any cars on it, and then, suddenly, I find myself catching up to a whole pack of them. That's when I have to figure out whether I can maneuver through the pack or not.

The interstate is a strategy game. One misstep can lead to an accident. One time I had a doctor's appointment to make that I was late for. The appointment was on a school day, and the doctor's office was twenty-five miles from my school. As I was hurrying along on the interstate, I looked up and saw an exit sign. From reading the sign, I knew my exit was only two miles away. *I'm going make it,* I thought.

Ahead of me was a semi truck, which wasn't going very fast. I then looked at the left-hand lane and saw a car in it. The car in that lane did not seem to be going too fast either.

I then looked to the right hand lane and saw it was open. I had to make a decision. Should I take my chance of going in the left hand behind the car and hope it'll go fast enough so I can get ahead of the truck and quickly merge into the far right hand lane? Or should I go in the right hand lane and get ahead of both the semi-truck and the car lagging in the left hand lane?

I checked again to make sure the right lane was clear and then I moved into the lane. This was a simple decision to make, but there have been other, more difficult circumstances, when there were a lot of cars, and it was hard to determine which lane would go faster. Quick, logical, and strategic thinking is what is needed in order to be a clever driver on the interstate.

A parking lot is a similar matter, although most drivers usually don't travel at eighty miles an hour there. The thing I've noticed every time I drive in a crowded parking lot is that people act as if they're the only ones there. Whenever I drive up and down the lanes at a mall to find a parking spot, pedestrians just walk right out in front of me.

Once, when I was driving up a lane at a crowded Wal-mart, two women were strolling down the middle of the lane. There was no way I could get around them, so I flicked my lights at them to alert them that I was coming up the lane. They moved aside, but one of them shook an angry fist at me.

I understand that cars have to stop and yield for pedestrians at a crosswalk, but it's not logical for people to walk down the middle of a lane where cars drive up and down. As a person with Asperger's, it makes me anxious when a car suddenly backs out of a parking spot or a pedestrian walks out right in front of me. From my experience driving on interstates and in parking lots, I learned that other people don't always obey the rules. That's why it is essential to be a vigilant driver.

YOUR PARENTS ARE THE BEST MENTORS

Your parents should explain more in-depth details about driving. Ask them for advice and always be with them while you're a novice driver. When I started driving, I hardly knew the difference between the gas and brake pedals. My mom, however, has over thirty years of experience. I have to admit that it can be a pain, for my mom was telling me to "Slow down" or "Honk your horn" at times, but I always felt safer with her in the car.

One day, my mom allowed me to drive her up to an outlet mall. The nearest one is fifty miles away from where we live, forty of which are on the interstate. The way up to the outlet mall wasn't much of a hassle, but we ran into some congestion on the way back home.

Many cars—some smaller, and some bigger than her Mountaineer—were flying past me and compacting into little groups. It was hard to get around them. There was one point where two semi-trucks took up two out of three expressway lanes. The car that was in the other lane was not in much of a hurry.

"Get behind the semi in the middle lane," my mom told me.

"Why?" I asked her. "Semi-trucks go slow."

"Just do it, Jeff."

I checked to make sure the lane was clear and then I moved into it. About five miles later, we were ahead of the pack.

"How did you know that the one semi would go the fastest?" I asked her.

"Well, the car that was hogging the fast lane wasn't going to budge from his spot and neither was the other semi," she explained. "The one semi wanted to get ahead of the other."

She went on to say that semi-trucks are allowed to pass other vehicles, but they can't hog up the whole roadway. From her quick decision-making and her knowledge of driving, we did not get stuck in the pack for too long. This may have been a lucky guess, but nonetheless, it was a guess based on experience.

Driving is a complex skill. It cannot be learned from a textbook, only through experience. It requires much planning ahead, abstract thinking, and multi-tasking. If you don't feel up to driving, or if it's not the thing for you, there's nothing wrong with not driving.

Several acquaintances of mine who are seventeen years and older don't drive. There are other forms of transportation out there besides driving, like buses, or carpooling with family or friends.

Note to Parents: *You're the Decision-maker*

"Oh no! My child is going to drive! What should I do?!" I think most parents feel this way when their child gets behind the wheel of a car. It is a huge responsibility for your AS teen to take on. Your Asperger's teenager can learn this skill, but it is ultimately up to you to decide if he or she is able to take on such a responsibility.

Only when you feel your Asperger's teen has earned this privilege and has demonstrated that he understands the responsibility that accompanies driving, should he learn to drive. But a privilege can easily be taken away if misused. If you feel that your AS teen has become a reckless or incompetent driver, never be afraid to take his license away from him. Thousands of teens end up in automobile accidents world-wide each day. Make sure that doesn't happen to your son or daughter.

As for whom your Asperger's teenager should learn to drive with—it should most definitely be you. When my parents taught me to drive, I felt more relaxed and motivated to be a safe driver. Train your AS child to be an effective and defensive driver.

If she makes an error when starting to drive, don't yell at her. When I made a minor mistake, like turning too sharply, or if I were driving too slowly, my mom would shout "Stop going so fast!" or "Speed up!"

Every time she shouted at me, I would momentarily panic and some-times mentally shut down. This has happened only on a few occasions, but whenever I was yelled at, I thought that I was a bad driver and not worthy to be on the road.

I'm not saying your AS teenager will have a meltdown or panic if yelled at, but it could very well discourage her interest in driving and will possibly cause her to view driving as something dangerous and not fun There's nothing wrong with being stern about teaching your Asperger's teen to drive, but don't yell at her. When I drove with my dad, he never yelled. Instead he calmly made his point when I made a mistake.

Another thing you should never do is grab hold of the steering wheel. My mom has done this in the past to keep me from making an error. I know she does whatever she can to help me, and I bless her for that.

But a few years ago, I heard a story about a passenger who caused an accident by grabbing hold of the driver's steering wheel. As a result, several people died. This is a drastic story, but it could happen. Never, ever grab the steering wheel while your AS teen is driving, unless you're helping her when she is first learning to drive. And do this only in a safe location, such as a neighborhood. You may think you're helping, but you could very well be doing the exact opposite.

GETTING THE LICENSE

I waited to get my license until after my sophomore year in high school. I thought at the time that it would be best to wait until school was out. The nearest license bureau was more than ten miles from where I live. When my parents called the bureau to set up an appointment for my final driving test, we learned that it was booked up all the way into the latter part of the summer. Apparently, many people thought as I did.

I didn't want to wait that long, so my mom found another license bureau that was a little farther away, but wasn't overwhelmed with appointments. So my mom set an appointment there for the late part of the spring.

I was a little anxious when the date came around for my final driving test at the bureau, but I felt certain I would do well and receive my license that day. I had prepared for it well over six months.

The final test was broken into two parts, maneuverability and driving. I was most worried about the maneuverability part of the test. A lot of kids who had gotten their license said that it was the most difficult part. Despite feeling somewhat intimidated, I still felt confident that I would ace it, and I did.

But the driving part of the test was something else, because I had no idea that it involved driving through a town, stopping and starting at countless red lights and stop signs, and there was one point where I had to cross several lanes of traffic to get to the other side of the road. It was mentally exhausting, and really put my driving skills to the test.

My tester gave me no warning of where and when he wanted me to make a turn, much less about where to drive. There was one point during the test where he wanted me to make a left at a red light. Well, I couldn't get into the left lane because a bunch of cars were hogging that lane. So I had to straddle a lane in order to get into the left-hand lane.

Bottom line, I flunked the driving part of the test. I was so worried about the maneuverability part that I had not even imagined such a difficult driving course. Learning that I had failed my first driving test shocked me. The many mistakes I had made really tallied up. I was disappointed with myself.

Besides not knowing the area of the driving course very well, my biggest error was letting my confidence get in the way of my driving. At seventeen, I thought I was the best driver in the world. Less than a year of driving, however, hadn't made me an expert driver.

Several weeks later, I took the driving test again at a different location and passed it. Driving tests can be intimidating, but you can prevail. What helped me pass my second driving test was a simple list of tips that I had come up with from my experience of failing the previous one.

Before taking the test, ask the tester as many questions as you need. The instructor for my first driving test would not let me ask any questions as I drove. At one point, when I was making a turn, I asked him if his side was clear. For years, my mom had asked me whether or not my side was clear when she was going to make a turn. I had developed this as a habit.

To my surprise, the tester said, "Why don't you look for yourself?"

I looked to the right and saw it was clear, but when I turned my head to look at the left, there was a swarm of cars coming. Quickly, I hit the gas pedal and pulled out in front of the flow of traffic. When I made this move, a slight sign of horror crossed my tester's face.

Be relaxed and mild-mannered. I was a bit on edge with my first driving test. My tester kept telling me, "You're sweating, relax." I think I gave him the impression that I was nervous every time I was behind the wheel of a vehicle, and that's one impression you don't want to give your tester. They don't like fidgety and nervous novice drivers. That's why before my second driving test I took some deep breaths and stretches.

If it is possible, try to find a sensible tester. Some instructors can be opinionated, bland, or impatient. My first tester was rather color-less and austere in his opinions and responses. However, the instructor I had for my second driving test was very courteous. She smiled and did not tell me to turn onto a road at the last second. Instead she gave me a few seconds' notice of a turn she wanted me to make. I felt more relaxed around her.

I didn't know the area very well for my first driving test. For my sec-ond shot at it, I drove around the town where the license bureau was located. This made me a better judge of the roads, the flow of traffic, and other obstacles that could cause penalties on a driving test. I suggest you drive around the area where you will take the test so you can get a feel for what the course may be like.

Watch out for stop signs. If you don't stop at the stop sign, you'll lose points. I learned that the hard way on my first driving exam, when I stopped five feet ahead of everyone else so I could see around a curb or any other obstacle. If you stop at a stop sign and you can't see around it, ask permission from the tester so you can creep up and get a clearer view of the road. This lets your tester know you are conscientious about your driving.

Be courteous. When I completed my second driving test, I undid my seat belt and opened my door.

"Where are you going?" my tester asked me.

I told her that I was going to open her door for her. Flattered, she said I was sweet, but that she could get it on her own. If you have a female tester, open the door for her. She'll see that you are respectful, and you may earn some bonus points. I didn't earn any bonus points, but I got a compliment.

OTHER HELPFUL TIPS IN GETTING YOUR LICENSE

1. Pay attention. Do what the tester says.
2. Be well groomed. The first impression is the only one they'll get of you.
3. After you finish the test, listen to what the instructor has to say

to you about your driving. Then thank him for his time riding with you.

For those of you who are preparing for your driving test, good luck! I hope these hints will come in handy.

DIRECTIONS

To get to a location, I need to decide on which route is the quickest and safest to take. I also need to make sure I know where I'm heading so I won't get lost. In the past, I used to carpool with a friend of mine to get to church. After I got my license, I chose to drive on my own. I felt that I knew the route to get there from my home.

On that following Sunday I readied myself for church and headed out the door. I was about two miles away from the church when I made an early right turn at a red light. About a mile down the road, I came to realize that the scenery and the road itself were different. Then I knew I had made an error.

Since I was on a road that I wasn't familiar with, I was scared. As I traveled along the road, I looked to see if there were any places on the side where I could make a U-turn. There was nothing but farms. I then checked to see if anyone was behind me. Sure enough, there was a line of cars.

I had no other option but to keep driving until I either found a place to pull over and turn around, or got to an intersection where I could make a U-turn. Three miles later, I came upon a red light. I got in the left-hand turn lane and waited for the light to change. When it did, I pulled as hard a left as I could, and drove back down the road going the opposite direction. I got to the church just a few moments before the elder began his sermon. I was even luckier to find a parking spot.

There were some instances in this experience when I had the urge to panic, but I kept myself calm. Getting overwhelmed and losing the ability to focus while driving is not an option. It's scary getting lost while driving. After this incident, I always make sure I know where I'm going and, if need be, have directions.

For my junior and senior years of high school, I transferred to a new school. During the summer before my junior year, I practiced driving to the new school with my mom to familiarize myself with the routes I could take, as well as the area. Familiarizing yourself with roads is an important skill. If you need a navigational system to help get you around places, then I suggest you get one. I never needed one, but it came in handy during one spring break, when my mom and I drove to Florida.

It told us a few miles in advance when we needed to make turn and what routes to take. After a daylong haul, the navigational system got us to our destination. In addition to using the navigational system, we used the state maps to see what alternate routes we could take to get to our destination.

Another option that could be beneficial is using online instructions from a website like MapQuest. I have to say, though, that MapQuest has its inaccuracies. Years ago, my dad and I drove up to Amish country to get some furniture. The directions from MapQuest helped us a lot until we got on the last road.

The directional guide we had printed off the website said to make a left turn on a road and go on it for two miles. After those two miles, the furniture store would be on the right. We traveled on the road for two miles and there was no store in sight. In fact, there was nothing but fields on either side of the narrow road.

"Are you sure the directions said to turn on this road?" my dad asked me.

"Yes."

"Did it say we were to turn left?" my dad then asked.

"Yes," I said, reading the directions carefully.

We drove an additional three miles and stopped at a gas station to get proper directions. The guy at the cash register said we were on the right road, but we went the wrong way on it. It ended up that the store had relocated a couple of years earlier.

"MapQuest needs to update its information," my dad grumbled when we finally got to the store.

If possible, find out how accurate and up-to-date an online resource or navigational system is. Always be sure that you know how to get to your destination. If you don't want to use a navigational system or trust online instructions, then ask someone you know who might give you instructions on how to get to the location, or use a map.

CELL PHONES

The first trip I ever made on my own was to return a couple of DVDs to Hollywood Video. After I entered the store and handed them to the cashier, I trotted off to my truck. I was thinking that everything would go all right. I got in my truck and put my keys in the ignition. The car's engine came to life. As I tried to pull the vehicle out of park into drive, the gearshift wouldn't budge. I put my foot on the brake and pulled on it hard, trying not to break the darn thing. It still would not budge. Then I knew I had a problem.

I looked around for my cell phone, but I couldn't find it. As many horrifying thoughts went through my mind, I became frantic. I was phoneless, and my car would not change gears. What was I going to do? I ran back inside the store and sheepishly asked the cashier to borrow the phone so I could call my dad.

"What did you do?" my dad demanded when I told him that my car wouldn't start.

"I-I don't know," I stuttered. "When I got to the store, I put my car in park, and turned it off. I walked into the store to return the DVDs—and when I came back to turn it on, it wouldn't shift."

He sighed. "All right, I'll be there in fifteen minutes."

After what felt like forever, dad came to my rescue. It turned out that I had not put my car in park after all. I had only moved the shift gear further than neutral on the dashboard, but not totally into park. Because my car was not in gear, it stalled. My dad managed to put it into park, then reverse, and backed it out of the parking spot. I was relieved and fortunate.

In case of any emergency, whether your car breaks down or you're lost, always have a cell phone. It is a lifeline. From this incident, I learned that forgetfulness was not an option.

OTHER PASSENGERS

You may at times have one or more passengers with you when you're driving. I have given lifts to family members and even some fellow classmates after school. In my junior year, I gave a girl a lift a couple of times a week for a few months. I enjoyed giving her rides home, but after a few months it got rather burdensome.

She wanted to do stuff with me after school, like hanging around at my house. I had no problem with that. But soon, she wanted me to give her a lift every day. There are some days after school that I have things to do, like my volunteer hours at the hospital, doctor's appointments, and other matters.

I tried to explain to her that there were days that I had other things to do, but she would persuade me not to do them. I felt that she was becoming a leech. Our casual friendship had turned into her obsession.

One time as I was driving her home, she said, "Oh, Jeff, can we get some food?"

"It's almost four o'clock," I told her.

"Yeah, but I'm hungry," she replied.

"Well, I'm going to be getting dinner soon," I said.

"Oh, can I come?" she inquired.

I was trying to drive and at the same time trying to tell her that I was told by my mom and her parents to take her straight home. As a person with AS, it's hard for me to talk and drive at the same time.

A bit irritated, I said, "I can't talk right now. I need to focus on driving."

She huffed. "Oh, come on."

We ended up going through a McDonald's drive-thru before I got her home. After the second month of giving her lifts, I felt worn out. I talked to my mom about it.

"I like her, but I feel under her control," I explained to her. "I feel more like a big brother rather than her friend. I can't do that."

My mom understood. So she called the girl's mom, and they talked. My mom told me that the girl I was giving lifts to had a lot of things going on with school and her family. Her mom and my mom decided it would be best for me to distance myself from her. My time of being a chauffeur was over.

It's a common thing in high school for teen drivers to give other teens rides home. If you ever give someone else a lift, you must ask parental permission before you even consider it. It is a good deed to give someone else a ride home, but you should have permission to do so.

However, even if you do have permission to give someone a ride home, I would be a little cautious. People, particularly friends, can be influential. Some teenagers are very immature, and a lot of times they don't follow the rules of right and wrong. When driving, the driver is in control.

When chauffeuring someone, try not to get too engaged in a conversation with them, particularly if you are a novice driver. For my first year of driving, I did not like to talk and drive at the same time. I needed to give the road and traffic my undivided attention. Now, with more than two years of driving experience, I am more relaxed about talking while driving. But I still keep my full attention on driving.

If there comes a time where a passenger gets too distracting, let them know that they need to be quiet so you can concentrate on driving. They should understand. Caution comes first.

Chapter 8

Learning Language

For a long time, I've struggled with language. Grasping communication skills such as body language, metaphors, slang, idioms, the pronunciation of certain words, and understanding people's vocal tones is like trying to understand a foreign language. With such disadvantages, it was a struggle to blend with my school peers.

I always felt alienated and was considered the "weirdo" in school. As much as I've tried blending in, I usually end up humiliating myself. There are times I feel that I can't understand what other people are saying or even what emotions they're expressing.

When I was six or seven, my grandfather always teased me. He would constantly tell me, "You're pulling my leg."

I would say to him, "No, I'm not."

He would laugh and persist with his jokes and strange old sayings. Often, I would get hostile to the point that I'd walk up, pull his leg, and shout, "I'm pulling your leg! Are you happy?!"

Another time, in grade school, I got myself in deep trouble over calling a kid a name. When my mom picked me up from school, she warned me that I was "on thin ice."

I asked her, "Where's the ice? It's not snowing outside is it?"

That made her even angrier and, because of that, she added more time to my sentence of being grounded. These are examples of something called *figurative language*. My seventh grade Language Arts teacher defined figurative language as "Words describing something through the use of unusual comparisons. These comparisons are used to gain effect, interest, and creativity."

It is common for people with AS to have difficulty understanding figurative language. Whenever someone uses sarcasm, metaphors, or idioms, I take them literally. Since I'm a literal thinker, understanding figurative language can be difficult, for it is *not* intended for literal interpretation.

Now that I'm older, and after hearing them over and over, I understand the point of most of these idioms and metaphors. However, there are times I still don't understand some of the old sayings that my parents use. I have AS and am a logical thinker, but that doesn't make me a dummy. It took me a long time to realize that I don't have to feel like an oddball because I can't understand an old saying or an idiom.

Usually if I don't understand a phrase or an idiom someone uses, I try to have the courage to ask what that person means. The one phrase my mom would always use every time I got angry was "mad as a hatter."

I would always ask her, "Who's mad?" or "What's a hatter?" The only source I could come up with for the phrase was the Mad Hatter from *Alice in Wonderland*. Bothered by the meaning of the phrase, I one day finally asked her what the phrase "mad as a hatter" really meant.

She explained to me that a hatter is a person who makes and sells hats. In the old days, an element called mercury was used to make hats. Mercury was known for causing people physical impairment and insanity. I had never heard that mercury had once been used to make hats.

It is interesting to know the source and meanings behind metaphors and idioms. If you ask someone what an old phrase or saying means, you could learn something new.

SLANG, TEEN TALK, AND BODY LANGUAGE

I hear slang at school almost every day from my peers. "Hey Homie" or "What's up, dog?" are just some of the slang phrases, and teen talk that I hear girls chant at the mall, or guys shout in the school hallways.

A few years ago, a kid said to me, "What's up dude?"

I looked up and saw the ceiling.

"The ceiling," I replied.

He laughed. "No really, what's up?"

"The ceiling," I repeated.

This conversation didn't go very far, and the kid probably thought I was being a wise guy, since I was telling him that the ceiling was "what's up." I have noticed that a lot of teenagers at school use many different words and keep mixing them up and changing them. After hearing a new word or phrase, I'd sometimes say it to another teen, and they would understand what I was saying when I didn't. Many times I feel as though I'm on another planet.

Lately, when I hear a new word or phrase, I will look up the word or words in a dictionary to try to gain an insight into their meaning. According to my *Intermediate Dictionary,* the majority of the words that I've heard teens use either have a definition that doesn't make sense, or have no definition at all.

A kid in my tenth grade study hall would always use the word *grit* in every other sentence.

"What's up, grit?" he would always greet a friend of his.

What the heck is a grit? I looked up the word in my dictionary and came up with only two reasonable definitions.

- A small hard particle like sand
- Firmness of the mind or spirit

I also read somewhere that *grits* was an oatmeal-like breakfast. Well I don't think he was talking about eating oatmeal, sand, or having "firmness of the mind and spirit."

As with figurative language, slang is not based on literal meanings or interpretations. Again, because I have AS, I'm a logical, concrete thinker. Such a thought process can affect the ability to understand body language and verbal communication.

I can't translate body language any better than I can interpret slang. I'm absolutely illiterate when it comes to reading hand and body gestures, eye motions, facial expressions, and postures. I read in an article that body language expresses the majority of people's emotions, feelings, and attitudes.

When someone sighs, that person could be sighing for many different reasons such as irritation, relief, or exhaustion. It's hard for me to determine why a person may be sighing. Sometimes when I'm speaking to someone, that person could be telling me one thing, but his or her body language could be saying something totally different.

A while back, I used to talk a lot to a girl who I had a crush on. When she spoke, she sounded sweet and seemed interested in me. But I later found out that she didn't like me at all and was just pretending to like me. One time I asked her out to a movie.

"Oh, I-I can't," she said. "I-I got baby-sitting to do."

"Baby-sitting on a Friday night?" I asked her.

"Yeah," she replied.

I was focusing on what she said, rather than examining her body language. A person's body language could be saying something totally different.

In my late teen years, I came to see that girls have more elaborate and complex body language than guys do. Whenever girls gather at a table in the cafeteria or pack together in a circle, they're busy flicking their hair, rolling their eyes, and giggling.

For you male AS readers, does this behavior of girls absolutely exasperate you? I'm not trying to antagonize you female AS readers. I like girls, but sometimes I just don't get them. You may likewise feel frustrated with boys.

Understanding the subtext of body language can be tricky. What has helped me comprehend what a person is saying, or knowing how they're feeling, is to ask that individual something like "Is that what you said?" "Is this what you meant by that?" or "Are you all right?"

Usually that person says, "Yes," or "No, I mean that." This is a good mechanism to use so you can learn what a person really means by what he says, and more or less know what he's really feeling.

VOCAL TONES AND MISUNDERSTANDINGS

Since I'm inept when it comes to reading body language, I also get people's emotions and vocal tones mixed up. One time I went to the theater to see a movie with a friend of mine. I was in line at a concession stand, and a young couple was standing right behind me.

As I was deciding on what to eat and drink for the film, the lady behind me said in an elevated tone, "Will you hurry up, we're gonna be late for the movie!"

I froze like a statue. I felt that I was angering her, so instead of deciding what to buy, I left the line and made my way to the film with my head bowed. I felt ashamed and abashed.

To my surprise, the young man of the couple suddenly approached me as I was trotting away and said with an equally loud tone, "Hey, what's wrong, buddy?"

"Nothing," I said, startled by his sudden appearance. "I was making you guys mad and decided to move along."

"We were just playing with you," he said.

We ended up having a conversation about the different movies that were out in theaters that year. From my viewpoint, people who talk loud are yelling, and this gives me the idea that they are angry.

My mom is a person who can talk loud. I frequently tell her to "calm down." This only inflames her mood. Even if my mom isn't yelling, just laughing or talking loud, I'll still say, "Calm down" or "Chill out."

If someone's voice is very quiet, I assume that something is bothering them. There was a girl in my eighth grade English class who was always very quiet and at times she seemed lonely and sad. I would repeatedly ask her if something was wrong or if there was something I could do to cheer her up. She would shake her head and say, "No, I'm fine."

People with AS can misinterpret people's vocal tones very easily. A lot of times when I misinterpret someone's vocal tone, as in the case at the movie theater with the young couple, I usually freeze up like an overloaded PC. It's a defense mechanism I have. There have been other times, though, when I would react with retaliation, particularly when my mom would speak very seriously about an important issue.

"Jeff, you can't be so stressed over school," my mom once told me after I'd had a bad day at class.

"Are you mad at me for feeling this way?" I asked her.

"Now why would you ask a question like that?" she inquired.

"Well, are you?"

"No," she replied.

"Are you sure?" I persisted.

"Yes," she said with a slight sign of irritation.

She and I have had conversations about who was angry and who was the aggravator. It sounds a bit hysterical, but I'm befuddled when it comes to figuring out people's vocal tones. Another problem I have with verbal communication is saying things that may come out as rude or can be interpreted by others as harsh.

A few years ago, my grandfather died from cancer. When he was suffering, my family was on the rocks. One of my younger cousins kept getting emotional about him. So I once said to her, "I hope he dies sooner rather than later."

This enraged her. She ranted and raved at me, calling me "heartless" and "unsympathetic." I was shocked by her outburst.

"Why would you say such a thing?" she demanded.

"It is simple," I replied. "I don't want to see him suffer any more. He's a man who's meant to stand tall and proud like a Caesar, but he's stuck in bed, probably for the rest of his life. It appalls me. That's why I said it; because I'd rather seem him rest in peace than suffer excruciating pain."

Her anger increased, and I had to do some explaining to my family about my "heartless" attitude. I wasn't trying to sound cruel. I just have a tendency to say things that come out wrong, which can be misinterpreted as rude. My mom told me shortly after this event that I lack "being tactful."

"What is being tactful?" I asked her. "A new type of Tic Tacs™?"

She laughed. "No. You lack empathy towards others, which often leads you to give unintentionally offensive and insensitive remarks."

On the contrary, ever since I was little, my parents have taught me to always be polite to others, and I follow that rule very closely. Since I've been taught to be a courteous individual, I wondered how I could say such nasty things.

In my junior year of high school, I made a fifteen-minute narrative project on the Black Dahlia murder case for my Digital Design class. After completing the project, I sat down with my family and watched it. After seeing the first two minutes of the movie, I realized from my narration that I have a dry monotone. I was rather surprised that my voice wasn't colorful or animated, like my mom's. I can usually tell by her tone of voice when she's angry, sad, or is experiencing some other emotion, even when her voice is a bit elevated.

Unfortunately though, not everyone is animated with his or her voice. In fact, most people I have met have very tepid tones. My dad has a dry monotone. It's hard for me tell whether he's mad, tired, sad, or even happy. Almost every day, I have to ask him, "How are you feeling?" to know his actual mood.

Such a dry tone of voice makes it hard for other people to know if I am being sarcastic, serious, angry, or even happy. It is hard for me to understand other people's tones of voice and deduce their meanings.

There's no way I can change my normal tone, unless I change my voice to that of Master Yoda. And I don't think people could stand me if I spoke like him all day long. I don't know what I sound like when

I speak. That's why I often ask people when I talk to them how they perceive my words and tone of voice.

Likewise, if you don't understand a person's tone, it would be wise to ask that person to verify that you have not only understood what they said, but also how they meant it. If you feel that person is being sarcastic, ask him if he is. Hopefully, he will give you an honest answer.

Note to Parents: Speech

I enjoy expanding my knowledge of the English language by learning new and different words. I may spell words correctly and read them properly but I've had a past history of pronouncing some of them strangely. When I was little, I was credited as the clown of my family. When someone would say *whirlpool* I would say, "worm pool." When someone would say *mile per hour*, I'd say "mile per nour."

Many people with AS have speech problems such as stuttering, mumbling, and mispronouncing words. Usually such speech issues hit a person with AS in early childhood and, in many cases, AS individuals grow out of such problems.

I pronounce most words properly compared to when I was a small child, although I have tendency of saying words quickly, which at times I pronounce incorrectly. One word I still have some difficulty pronouncing is "with." I often say *wif* rather than "with."

Speech difficulties vary with each individual. If your Asperger's child has troubles with speech, I suggest you have a speech therapist help him or her. Back in my kindergarten and grade school days, I had a speech therapist who taught me how to pronounce my words properly and speak clearly. Not only would I say words incorrectly, but I was also prone to mumble.

Every time I entered my kindergarten class, my teacher would always heartily greet me. "Hello Jeff, how are you doing?" or "Isn't it a lovely day out today?" she would say. I would respond with a shy "hello" or a mumbled "I'm all right, thank you." Rather than lingering by her, I would walk away from her and sit at my desk with my head bowed.

Not only was I a shy kid, but I was also embarrassed by my speech problems. With speech therapy, I was able to return polite and casual responses. By the end of the year, I was able to talk to my teacher without mumbling or making many mispronunciations.

If your AS child has trouble with speech, it's best for him or her to have speech therapy in the early years, as I did. This way, your son or daughter will not have to be concerned with further speech impairments and be a target for bullying because he or she speaks differently.

Note to Parents: *Be Clear about What You Say*

Whenever I interrupt my parents, my mom often says to me "Jeff, wait for five minutes."

"Okay," I would say.

Then I would quickly find the nearest clock and see what time it was. I would watch it steadily for five minutes. When exactly five minutes passed, I would run back to my parents and say, "Okay, five minutes have passed."

I did this frequently to my parents when I was a small child. My intent was not to irritate them but to warn them that their time was up. What you say, parents, determines what action your AS child takes and how he perceives your words. If my parents gave me a specific time frame, I would abide by it. To prevent me from irritating them, my parents learned not to do this.

"Give us a few minutes, will you Jeff?" my dad would say.

"What's a few minutes?" I would then ask.

"Just wait Jeff, give us some time." My dad would add, "We'll call your name when we're finished talking."

I quickly got the idea that my parents needed their time away from me to get their "adult stuff" done. It could not always be about me. I'm not saying you should avoid giving specific time frames or details; sometimes they can be beneficial.

Every time my mom needed me to find her cell phone, she would say, "Look on the downstairs counter" or "Look in the butler's pantry." I would head precisely to those locations to search for her phone.

You have to be clear on what you say to your AS child. My parents always asked me if I understood them or if I needed more clarification. You also need to make sure your AS child understands what you have told them. Don't assume that your AS kid will automatically understand what you say.

"Jeff, are you sure you know where the envelope is?" my mom asked me one time when we were heading out on errands.

"Yes, upstairs, on your desk in the office," I said.

"Good. Go get it," she told me.

I ran upstairs to her desk in the office. As soon as I got there, I stared at her desk. I never thought I would see such a cluttered area of paper. I skimmed through all the papers and whatnots on her desk. I could not find the envelope she had described to me.

I must have been in her office for five minutes before I heard her voice from downstairs, "Did you find it yet? What's taking you so long?"

"I can't find it," I hollered down to her.

"It's on the desk."

"I can't find it."

"Don't make me come up there!" she shouted.

"I'm telling you, I can't find it; your desk is cluttered!"

"Jeff, I swear, you can't find a pole even if it's right in front of you!" I then heard her run up the stairs. When she entered the office she grabbed the envelope off of the chair.

"There it was right in front of you!" she yelled, holding it close to my face.

"You told me to look on your desk, not your chair," I told her.

AS people follow *specific* instructions. If my mom had said "It's on the chair" then I would have found it. Make sure your Asperger's kid understands you, even if you have to repeat yourself a few times.

Note to Parents: *Eye Contact*

I generally don't look into a person's face when I talk to someone or when an individual talks to me. Usually my eyes drift over their shoulders or scan an object nearby. Most people I know consider this impolite.

My parents regularly tell me to look into a person's eyes when he or she is speaking to me, or when I am speaking to him or her. My parents call this showing respect, but I find it quite discomforting to look someone in the eyes. When I do, I feel like my eyes are on fire, and I need to pull away. It's almost as if my eyes were being hypnotized by an alien. I'm not trying to sound rude, but that's the way I feel about eye contact.

I no longer avert my eyes when someone speaks to me. Rather, I look people in the face. But I usually don't look into a their eyes, but at their lips or mouth. If I am in a conversation, I occasionally make momentary eye contact, but then turn my gaze back to their mouth.

When people talk to me, I often tend to focus on their appearance rather than what they are talking about. It's difficult for me to look at someone and listen to them at the same time.

Having eye contact is nearly impossible for people with Asperger's Syndrome, and it is common for them to look at a person's mouth or lips rather than the eyes while talking or being talked to (this was in Dr. Volkmar's study, mentioned in the first chapter of the book).

In my opinion, a person doesn't need to look people in the eyes, or in the face, for that matter, to listen to them when speaking. The best way to know if your AS child is listening to you is to ask a question that is relevant to the topic you're chatting about. This way you know for sure if he is paying attention or not. When someone doesn't look at you when speaking, it doesn't mean he is not listening.

Chapter 9

Bullying

Bullies usually like to pick on someone who is smaller or weaker than they are, but I had the advantage of being the tallest and biggest kid in school throughout my kindergarten and elementary years. However, bullies don't always hunt their victims just by appearances. I was a bully's target because of my social differences, and because I didn't blend in with the rest of the students.

In gym class, I was often ridiculed because I wasn't good at group activities like dodge ball or basketball. I never had the reaction speed or motor skills to catch or throw a ball. Rather than trying to catch a ball, I would do whatever I could to get out of its way, whether it was by ducking, shielding my eyes, or jumping out of its path. The boys would laugh and taunt me: "Big Jeff can't catch a ball. He's too scared."

The worst part of gym for me was when the teacher assigned students into groups. I would always be picked last, and the team I was placed in often moaned, "Sir, do we have to have him?" I would frequently avoid this humiliation by fleeing to the boys' bathroom, waiting in a stall until class was over.

Most of the bullies I have encountered were guys, but that doesn't mean girls can't bully, too. Back in the fifth grade, there was a girl whose sole mission seemed to be making my life miserable. It started when I was in an after-school program called Latchkey, which involved a place where kids could wait until they were picked up by their parents. The adults who ran the program often allowed us to go to the playground to play around. Since I never really liked playing outside, I would walk laps around the playground to get some exercise and alone time.

As I was making my laps one day, I heard a voice ask, "What are you doing?"

I looked up and saw a girl standing in front of me.

"I'm walking," I replied.

"Oh, can I join?" she asked.

"I'd rather be alone right now," I said.

"Why?" she asked.

"I just want to be alone," I said. "Is that a problem?"

"Oh, so you don't like girls?" she said, taking offense.

"No, that's not the point." I was quite uneasy.

"Then what is the point?" she demanded.

"Please, just leave me alone! I just want to be alone."

As I ambled away from her, I turned to look behind me and saw that she was *following* me. Feeling more anxious, I quickened my pace. She quickened hers.

I looked ahead and saw two kids who were looking at us. I heard one of them say to the other, "Get a teacher."

The next month or so I was consistently pestered and bothered by this girl. She would get in my face and begin asking questions like "What's your name?" "Where were you born?" or "Why are you always so quiet?"

There was one time when I was riding on a bus to Latchkey when she sat across the aisle from me. She jumped across into my seat and asked, "How old are you?"

She was so close to me that I could smell her breath.

"You're squishing me," I replied. "I won't be able to get out when the bus stops."

"Okay! Okay, you idiot!" she shouted.

This harassment wore me down. I finally sought a solution to this with the school principal. He solved the problem by having a chat with her before school one day. It turned out that she was a very troubled individual and that I was not the first person that she had harassed.

WHAT IS A BULLY?

There are in-depth reasons for why people bully. Most of these reasons are psychological. For instance, a kid might have an abusive family, or been abused by someone other than his or her family. It usually comes down to the bully having been bullied.[1]

It takes time and pressure for someone's mood to change, like rocks compressing and compacting underground to form new ones. Bullying is a vicious cycle. Bullies would rather take their rage and troubles out on someone else rather than confront their own issues. Such selfish and harmful actions make bullies hateful individuals.

Unfortunately, bullies like to target anyone they find who is different from them, whether it is in appearance or social difference. It's even worse when other kids follow such a troubled individual, as if they were his or her gang. That makes them cowards.

If someone says or does something that is hurtful, I see that person as a bully. Now I'm not proposing that saying something in a hurtful, obnoxious, or even in a teasing way, makes a person a bully. As a person with AS, it is hard for me to tell when a person is a bully and when they're not. In the hallways, I would often see boys tackling and kicking one another. After their brawl, they would laugh and go about their business. I find this very strange. Why would two people fight each other and then laugh about it as if it did not even happen? Teachers have come to call this "horseplay."

It is understandable that people get a little rough with each other in a "playful" fashion. My dad and I sometimes hit one another on the shoulder or slap one another over the head. None of it is serious, but it can cross the line when someone does this to an individual who doesn't want to be touched.

In my freshman year, there was a boy who kept knocking into me and shoving me. I told him to leave me alone and that I did not want to be touched, but he kept doing it anyway. Not understanding that he was goofing around, I took the horseplay seriously. When he came around trying to shove me again, I grabbed his arm and twisted it.

I got in a bit of trouble that day. The vice principal had to explain to me that I was prohibited from fighting with other kids in school. She also had to explain to the other boy that touching other students was forbidden.

Sometimes I see kids tease each other. In the fifth grade, other kids would often try to persuade me to sit with them at lunch. There were days I felt comfortable enough to sit with them, and I would, but there were other times I felt that I just wanted to be alone. I would say, "No, but thank you."

Kids would persist and say things like, "Come on Jeff, don't be a chicken," or "Don't be such a sourpuss." I often gave in. I felt that if I continued to say no, I would get more insults. It felt like a form of bullying, but it was just a way some students made me join their group.

As a person with AS, it is hard for me to tell when someone is or is not a bully. Reading facial expressions, understanding body language, and even comprehending tones of voice is difficult for me. For certain though, there'll never be a person who would walk up to you and say, "I'm going to bully you from now on." It doesn't happen that way.

To know if someone is bullying me, I often speak up and address the person who shoved me or called me a name I find unpleasant. Speaking up has usually helped my situations. If it did not, then I involved other people, such as my parents and school faculty. But a simple act of horseplay or mild name-calling does not necessarily make someone a bully.

Back with the kid in the ninth grade who shoved me, it was not necessarily an act of bullying. The kid did not know that I was someone who did not like to be touched. I didn't know that his shoving me was a form of horseplay. People's actions can be easily misunderstood, but telling the person that you're not comfortable with their actions can easily end a situation whether it is just horseplay, or even bullying.

DAMAGE BULLIES CAN INFLICT

I have briefly acknowledged in earlier chapters that I developed paranoia in the eighth grade. It all started with a bully. In my English class, I noticed a kid who, every time he looked at me, would whisper something to a pal next to him and they would both laugh. I had no clue as to what he had said, but to my mind it didn't look good.

I did not take it seriously at first, but I kept my eye on him. Every other time I would turn and look at him in class, I saw him once again looking at me, whispering something in a dude's ear and they'd chuckle. After a little while, I got tired of this.

One day after my English class ended, I went to the principal's office. I told the principal what I had witnessed and gave him the student's name. The principal told me he would sort the matter out as soon as he could. The next day of school, the principal approached me in the hallway and told me that he had talked to the kid, and that he was spreading false rumors and saying untruthful things about me.

The principal assured me that the issue was taken care of and that there would be no problems with the other kid. I was gracious and I thanked him for his help. But that was only the beginning.

Because of this little incident, I had a fear of going to school every day that year. I thought each person I saw looking at me, or whispering and laughing, was saying bad things about me behind my back. Within a month's time, I had called half of the students in the school to the principal's office to find out if they were really saying harsh things about me or not.

None of it was true, but it all felt so real. It was hard to decipher what was real and what was in my head. I felt everyone was out to get me.

From my experience in junior high, bullies can do a lot of emotional and mental damage. Bullying can ruin a person's self-esteem, raise their anxiety levels, and make them lose interest in school, extracurricular activities, or developing friendships.

However, you don't have to let one incident pulverize your life. I wasted an entire school year because of my paranoid thoughts about being bullied. If you think someone is talking bad about you behind your back, but you're not sure, don't be afraid to ask them a question like "Excuse me, what did you say?" or "What are you talking about?" You would then know if they were talking about you or not. Anyone can be bullied, and it usually occurs unexpectedly, like a thief in the night, but you don't have to be a victim.

STANDING UP TO BULLIES

Besides the sick enjoyment of making their victims' lives miserable, bullies like to wield power over others and dominate them, like a tyrant.

From experience, I have learned that if you take that power away from them, it makes them fumble. A while back, a kid dared me to fight him.

I asked him, "Why would you want to fight me?"

He did not give an answer. I knew from his past inappropriate, and sometimes violent, behavior toward other students, that he was a mischievous individual. In the hallways, I had seen him tackle and fight students. He was also close to my size. As I looked at him, several kids gathered behind him. I felt quite nervous and afraid. Not only did the possible injuries I might sustain frighten me, but also how much trouble I might end up in if I did fight him. I kept my cool and reminded myself of the deep breathing techniques my physical therapist had taught me.

"I am going to kick your butt!" he said.

"Really?" I said. "I am over six feet tall, and two-hundred and twenty pounds."

"So?" he retorted.

"Do you know martial arts?" I then asked him.

"No," he said.

"I do," I replied. "I have three years experience, and I'm a black belt, first don. I know how to fight and, if need be, seriously injure a person with my bare hands."

He recoiled a bit.

I added, "Besides, what's the point in fighting anyway?"

I then walked away. I had some advantages, but I did not panic, nor did I lose my temper from that incident. I was polite and I did not retaliate. Most of the time if someone says something I find offensive, I ignore them.

One time when I was heading to my bus after school, a kid once pointed and shouted at me, "Look at that big retard!"

I had never spoken a word to him, or even seen him before, but he still made fun of me. His words were hurtful, but I did not retaliate or dwell on the matter.

In the fifth grade, I learned that returning an insult only inflames situations. As my sixth grade science teacher stepped out of the classroom, a kid from the other side of the room called me a "retard."

I looked up at him and shouted back, "And you're an a-hole!"

We exchanged insults with each other for several minutes. The teacher was not present as we shouted harsh words across the classroom. It went on until I couldn't bear it anymore. I fled from the classroom and ran down the hallway like a maniac, yelling, screaming, and crying, looking for any adult who might help. The principal had to separate us for the rest of that day. Retaliation only makes matters worse. It's a waste of time. Bullies are certainly not worth yours.

From experience, I know that bullies like to attack their victims when they're alone. Whenever I was a bully's target, I tried to remain close to the school staff. In the classrooms, I always sat at the desk closest to the teacher. At recess, I tried to stay in sight of one of the adult monitors.

Never hide in a corner or put yourself in a situation you can't get out of. There was a kid I knew back in the fifth grade who often hid in the restroom to escape from his predators. One day, as he hid in the bathroom, his bullies tracked him down and did horrible things to him. Always be in a place where adults are so they can help you, and never be afraid to ask for an adult's help.

Through my early school years, I was fearful to ask for help from adults because I didn't want to give them the impression that a big kid like me couldn't fend for himself. Other times I felt embarrassed because I thought that I might have brought the bullying upon myself because of my social differences. It's easy to feel guilty about something, but being attacked by a bully is never the victim's fault.

Never let yourself be a victim or feel that you must constantly look over your shoulder for a bully. Living with guilt and shame is not living at all. Bullies have a life, and they choose to be miserable with it. Don't let them influence you in any way.

Never be afraid to speak up if you're bullied. Being silent about it will only eat you up. I know; I've been there. They love to control others and make them miserable for their own amusement.

As Norm said in the old sitcom *Cheers*, "It's a dog-eat-dog world, and I'm wearing Milk Bone underwear." Don't be the one who wears Milk Bone underwear.

If a bully keeps harassing you even after a teacher or other adult has spoken to them, get help from the school's principal or guidance counselor. In the sixth grade, there was a kid who kept taunting me about my glasses. I constantly told him to leave me alone, and I even asked the teacher to solve the matter. When that didn't work, I turned to the principal to sort it out. That kid never bothered me for the rest of the school year.

If the principal or a guidance counselor doesn't seem able to solve the issue, get your parents involved. In the second grade, a kid kept taunting me with harsh words, and he would physically shove me and get into my face. I repeatedly asked the punk to leave me alone, but he never listened. I even brought it to the attention of some teachers, and he still did not give up his viciousness.

After several months of constant abuse, I told my mom to get involved. One day, after school at Latchkey as he was leaving with his mom, my mom and I confronted him. My mom told his mom what he had been doing to me. His mother was indignant. The matter was sorted out within a few moments, and he never bothered me again. Your parents know what's best.

If your parents or the school don't help, you might have to get law enforcement involved. I don't want to sound like Jack McCoy from the show *Law and Order*, but harassment and assault is considered a crime. There was one instance where a girl in the seventh grade assaulted me by placing a pair of scissors close to my eyes.

I asked her, "What do you want?"

"I want your lunch money," she demanded.

I felt threatened. I quickly slapped away her hand that held the scissors and got away from her as fast as I could. After the incident, I told the school resource officer what had happened. I told him who the girl was and what she looked like. The matter was sorted out quickly after he had a chat with her. Only do this as a last resort.

If need be, transfer to a different school to escape the viciousness of bullies. Since I transferred to a vocational school, I've had little trouble compared to my old high school.

Note to Parents: *How You Can Help*

Your AS child will not be able to solve all of his issues on his own. It was always hard for me to tell my parents that I had been bullied. I had a tendency to dwell on the matter instead of releasing it by talking to them about it.

When I'd come home from school on a day I had been bullied, my mom would ask, "How's your day?" It was hard for me to decide what to say and what not to say. I usually wouldn't bring it up automatically unless my mom or dad would specifically ask about it. And a lot of times, when I'd mention incidents of being bullied, they had happened too long ago to be worth notifying the school about. Your AS child also may not bring up such a sensitive issue.

If you just ask, "How's your day?"

Your Asperger's kid won't say, "I was bullied today."

It doesn't work that way. It can be difficult to tell whether something is upsetting your AS child or not. My mom could always tell something was wrong with me by my downcast eyes, or my lack of laughter or interest in a remark she would make.

"Jeff, did you know that they're now releasing Halo 3?" my mom asked me one time when we were having lunch at a restaurant. Like many other teens that I know, I think *Halo* is one of the best things invented since Christmas.

"Oh," I uttered.

"Why? You don't like Halo now?" she inquired.

"I do like it, but ..."

"But why?" she asked me.

I sighed. "I had a really bad day. Nothing has gone right."

I poured out my feelings to her about the chain of events that caused my bad mood. I had been persistently pestered in my lab over a camera, because it was taking longer than molasses in January to load my video footage on the computer, and kids in my Government class kept taunting me about my "fancy" I-POD.

To really know if something is bothering your AS child, ask what's vexing him and be specific with your questions. You should get an answer, whether it is about a bullying issue or something else.

OTHER HELPFUL TIPS FOR PARENTS

Do not go to the school and confront your kid's bully in front of everyone. Such an action will make the other kids view your AS child as a "momma's" or a "daddy's boy," and will only make the situation worse. There was a kid in fifth grade whose father came to the school to confront his son's bullies.

After the boy's father had left, the bullies laughed at him and asked, "That's your father? He looks like a bloody hobo!"

The poor kid's troubles only deepened.

To prevent this from happening to your AS child, I suggest you talk to your child's teachers and other school staff members about the issue. A few times in the past when I was bullied, my mom would meet with my teachers and the principal after school to find a way to sort the problem out. This is a great way to solve a bullying problem, but do this only after or before school, when it is private. Being a little secretive will make you anonymous, and your AS kid will feel safer.

If your Asperger's child is being bullied at school, and the affair hasn't been sorted out, don't send him there. This would be like throwing him into a fire pit. Don't make your AS child suffer in any form.

Home education or school transfer is always an option. I never was home schooled, but ever since I transferred to a new school, I have felt more secure and not so overwhelmed by the mean acts of the bullies at my old school.

SIDEBAR NOTE: TEACHERS, YOU CAN HELP, TOO

It's immensely difficult for someone, especially if that person has Asperger's Syndrome, to pluck up the courage to ask for help, particularly with regard to a bullying issue. I know it can be a rough world for kids, but it's not supposed to be, and especially not for a person with AS.

If an AS student has the strength to ask for your help, listen to her and see if you can help with the matter. Do not shrug it off or dismiss it. Every time I was bullied, I felt threatened. There was an instance in my junior History class when a girl claimed that I had "stolen her parking spot."

She told me that if I ever stole her spot again, she would key my truck. Well, there is no assigned parking at the school, and I don't pull into a person's spot when they're trying to back into it.

I brought it up to my history teacher who shrugged and said, "She won't key your car, Jeff."

Since he didn't help me, I turned to the principal. He assured me that he would have a talk with the girl. The next day, the principal approached me in the hallway, told me that the issue had been sorted out and I didn't have to worry about getting a new paint job for my truck.

Whichever tactic you choose to solve a bullying issue for a student, never announce to the class that so-and-so is being bullied and tell the general class to stop it. In the third grade, a teacher of mine did this after my pencils were stolen. I looked around the classroom and saw several boys at a table giggling and pointing at me. I was humiliated. Not only was it embarrassing, but it also made me more of a target. The issue only worsened when more of my pencils and papers disappeared.

Another thing I suggest you not do is roam about in the classroom and say, "I have no evidence of bullying" to the victim. Most of the bullies I have encountered don't misbehave in class in front of the teacher. If you really want to catch a bully, I suggest you be a little sneaky. Sneak up on them at their lockers or during lunch. Use the element of surprise.

CAN TEACHERS BE BULLIES?

Teachers can be bullies. Now I'm not saying teachers are bad. The teachers I have had in the past have been good, overall. Some teachers I've known have been willing to go out on a limb to help me out. But there are those teachers who are so strict and "by-the-book," that I think of them as hardheaded, and even mean.

I've always assumed that many of these teachers have not had an AS student in their class. Well, it's not an everyday thing to meet someone with AS, or even to know anything about it. Because of this, I believe that many teachers don't know how to react to or understand a student who behaves differently or has a different cognitive perspective than the normal batch of students.

One of the teachers I had trouble with was my computer teacher back in the seventh grade. At the start of the school year, she was really nice to me. She laid down all the rules, crystal clear. As an individual with AS, I like rules, and I abide by them.

The first rule in her class was that students were *not allowed to start working until she was done speaking*. One day, as she was addressing the class, a kid began mouthing off. She had to stop speaking to the class in order to discipline him. When she had to discipline that kid, I assumed that she was done talking and that it was time to start working. So I turned around to start my computer. She saw me turn on my computer and yelled at me.

I jumped in my seat. "What is it?"

"Why are you playing on your computer?" she demanded.

"I'm not," I said honestly. "I was just..."

"Demerit!" she barked.

I tried to explain to her that all I did was turn around to turn on my computer. She didn't bother to listen or give me the chance to explain myself. I felt she was directing her anger at the other student toward me.

When I persisted in clarifying my side of the story, she thought I was being argumentative. She misunderstood and threatened to give me two more demerits, which was equivalent to a detention. I gave up my defense and signed the demerit.

When I handed the demerit to her, she examined it and said, "You filled it out wrong."

"How?"

"You're supposed to sign for *three* demerits instead of one," she drawled.

"Why three? You said I had only one," I told her.

"Don't be a smart aleck," she snapped. "Three demerits!"

"You know, you're not making me feel very comfortable," I said, holding back my aggressive feelings.

"I don't care," she snarled.

I went back to my desk. Feeling angrier by the second, I re-signed the demerit, walked back to her desk, and handed it to her.

Every day I walked into her classroom, I prayed that I would not get yelled at because of some little mistake I might make. I felt even more anxious because in the seventh grade, trying to understand a computer was a challenge. I understood how to turn one on and log in, but I wasn't familiar with many programs of a PC. Microsoft Word was my only area of expertise back then.

The first project I had to do in that class was to create and present a

PowerPoint autobiography. I was confused by the program, and I had a dozen questions going through my mind. I did not want to ask the teacher because I was afraid that she would yell at me like the Queen of Hearts in *Alice in Wonderland*.

After several days of trying to figure out PowerPoint on my own, I gathered up the courage to ask the teacher a question. I got up from my chair, approached her desk, and asked, "Excuse me, can you help me with my project?"

She looked at me blankly. "Help you?"

"Yes, please," I said.

She sighed and leaned back in her chair. "Why don't you ask someone else for help?"

"But I thought it was your job to help," I said.

She glared at me. "One more remark like that from you, and I will give you a detention!"

I scurried back to my desk and stared at the clock until the bell rang for dismissal. I never thought that from one little incident, I would go from an acquaintanceship with a teacher to being seen as a problematic child. I thought of her as a bully, and she thought of me as a little devil. I would have done anything to get out of that class.

After a week of torture, my tolerance ran thin. I called for my mother's help. I told her what had happened, and that I was absolutely bitter about the computer class. My mom took action. She had a conference with the teacher and the school principal to work the issue out. My

144

mother told the computer teacher my side of the story of the incident, but she wouldn't listen, and made it sound as if I were the culprit.

My mom then tried to explain to her how I see things with my AS, and that when she stopped talking to discipline the other student, I had thought it was time to start working. Unfortunately, she wouldn't listen to that either. Because of the prejudice she had towards me, not only did she lose out on knowing me, but she didn't open her mind to learning about a kid with AS.

For the rest of the time I was in that class, my mom made sure I had an aide with me. With my aide present, I felt much safer and that I didn't have to worry about the teacher yelling at me. The aide was also there to help me with the projects I worked on in the class.

Some other teachers I have met liked to single out kids who have a disorder because they found them annoying. I knew a boy who was a special needs student, and who also suffered unkind words from his teachers because of his ADD. He was a forgetful and disorganized individual. I would always see his trapper keeper stuffed with papers, and his classroom books were never covered with book-covers.

One time, I saw two teachers standing next to each other, observing the hallways. As this boy was walking down the hall, "Oh, there he is, Mr. Forgetful. I swear, he can walk down this hallway with a pencil in his hand one second and it will be gone the next."

Then the other teacher laughed at her rude comment. I think many teachers believe that everyone should be "normal," and may find it impossible to accept someone who is different. When a teacher behaves in such a way toward a student with AS or any other mental challenge, it alienates them and makes them miserable. I find that to be very prejudicial.

I always thought of teachers as people to look up to and feel safe around, like a police officer. For you teachers who are reading this, I hope that you will open your mind and dismiss any prejudicial thoughts you may have against kids with AS or any other disorder.

TIPS FOR DEALING WITH TEACHERS WHO ARE BULLIES

If a teacher is abusing you in any way, tell him that he is upsetting you and that he should stop. If he doesn't listen and continues to harass you, keep calm and request permission to go to the principal's office.

Tell your parents about it and have them talk to the teacher.

Involve other school staff. Whenever I had trouble in my junior high years, I always sought help from the school's principal. Not only was the principal the boss of the school, but he was also a very good friend in helping me with issues involving school bullies.

If a teacher is still cruel to you after your parents have spoken to him or her, ask permission to have another adult in the classroom to supervise the teacher, or request permission to withdraw from that class. There was only one class I ever had to withdraw from, and that was my eighth grade science class.

All the assignments the teacher had us do were nearly impossible, and she wouldn't even bother to explain the material. Instead, she told us: "You're all in groups of four. I'm sure you can figure it out yourselves."

One day, I had the courage to ask her for help. When I did, she looked away from me and said, "Ask your group."

"But I have," I told her. "None of us knows what we're doing."

"It's all in the book," she said.

"Can you at least lend us a hand?" I pleaded.

She looked at me angrily. "Your group is either poor readers or slackers."

I then said, "I thought it was your job to help us."

"Five points are removed from your grade!" she screamed.

"But I ..."

"Want to make that ten?" she threatened.

I fled back to my group. To avoid her class, I would often retreat to the boy's restroom and wait for the bell to ring. She treated me so harshly that I was always afraid to go into her classroom.

When I came into her classroom the day after I had skipped a class, she would cross-examine me like an angry parent, "Where were you yesterday?"

I would always tell the truth. She would crack up and say loud enough for the entire class to hear, "You're such a retard, hiding in the boys' bathroom!"

I couldn't take it anymore. I remembered that my therapist had told me that if I wrote my feelings down on paper I could release a lot of stress. So, in class, I wrote down my feelings, which I have to admit were a bit extreme. After I had written my feelings down, I felt relieved. I crumpled up the paper just in time for the bell to ring. In a hurry to get to my second period, I ran out the door, leaving the crumpled paper behind on the desk. The next day of class, my science teacher called me up to her desk.

"Yes ma'am?" I asked.

"Follow me," she said. She led me into a back room that I had never seen before. As I entered the room, she closed the door and turned around, with a very red face.

"What is this?" she exploded, holding a wad of crumbled paper.

At the time, I did not know what she was talking about. I honestly replied, "I don't know."

"Oh don't give me that crap!" she yelled.

Feeling a bit nervous by this unwanted meeting, I said, "You're really making me feel uneasy."

"Good," she snarled.

She threw the wad of paper at me and added, "Why don't you read that?"

Then knew what she was talking about. It was the paper that I had written down my feelings on.

"You're so full of crap, you know that?" she then said. "You're so full of it!"

I said nothing.

After a very long moment, she finally said, "Get out of my class!"

My intention was not to upset her, but I couldn't take her abuse any longer. Halfway through the school year, I was removed from her class by permission of my mother, the junior high principal, and my psychiatrist. I was then placed in another science class with a new teacher.

A FINAL SUGGESTION

For three and a half years I was in karate. It's a difficult course that takes a lot of strength and physical endurance. Unfortunately, when I was ten, I had a bike accident that finished my karate days. Nevertheless, I felt that I had accomplished something worthwhile during the time I spent in it. I gained more self-confidence, motivation, perseverance, and a sense of pride.

In addition, I earned many medals, and achieved the high rank of a first don black belt, and my body was in good shape. I even had many acquaintances and friends at the dojo. I never felt that I stuck out like a sore thumb there.

Unlike football or baseball, Martial Arts is an individual physical activity. The only time I ever had to engage in a group was in sparring matches. And with learning martial arts, I did not have to be afraid of bullies. I knew how to defend myself if I ever got in an ugly situation.

Now I'm not saying you have to learn martial arts, but if you want to get in shape and know how to defend yourself, I highly recommend learning some form of it, whether it's judo, or tae kwon do, or karate. There are other individual physical activities you can do, too, like running track or lifting weights. Of course, lifting weights and running track doesn't provide self-defense skills, but they can get you in shape and help build inner strengths such as motivation, perseverance, and endurance.

I may not do karate anymore, but I still work out with weights and run. In my mind, there's nothing better than a good workout to build inner strength.

Chapter 10

Socializing and Friendships

Lacking social skills makes it very hard for me to get along with people and maintain friendships. Before any of you AS readers say that you don't want any friends, I think that is a common expression of loneliness. There are times I want to have friends, but at the same time I want to be alone.

There's nothing wrong with being alone. I enjoy my solitude at home. I try to spend it wisely, typing an assignment on my computer or working on several different manuscripts. Other times I like to lie in my bed, reading a good book or an interesting magazine article. But I've learned that being alone for a long time can make a person lonely and ill.

Friday used to be my least favorite day of the week. I would always come home from school, go to my room, close the door, and lie on my bed. I would stare at the ceiling and feel the isolation and loneliness build inside of me. There was no one to call, no one to hang out with.

No one. Nothing. I was quite despairing. Usually, my feeling of isolation dissipated by the time my parents came home from work, because then I was around people.

However, I did not always want to be around my parents. I wished to have a friend around my age. My wish was granted in the ninth grade when I met a sophomore who shares my AS condition.

He and I were so alike. We both enjoyed epic and foreign films, particularly oriental movies like *Hero* and *Yojimbo*. We both liked to play real-time strategy games and work with computers. We shared a study hall, and we often talked about tales of the samurai and Japanese anime. I felt accepted by him, and not like a foreigner or a "weirdo."

When the school year ended and it came time for summer break, we went a long time without seeing or talking to one another. I had his number written down on a piece of paper so I could call him, but unfortunately, I had misplaced it somewhere. I would search, tearing my room and computer desk apart to find it. I could not locate his number, and I got depressed because I missed his company. I then came to accept my loneliness.

When the loneliness started getting to me, I turned to the book that my grandfather had given me, called *Questions Young People Ask*. I skipped to the chapter that was on the topic of loneliness.

On page 115, it describes loneliness as "... a warning signal. Hunger warns you when you need food. Loneliness warns you that you need companionship. . . ." I read on in the chapter, and it gave me more answers that I sought. The first step in beating loneliness was by "trying to understand its cause."[1] I knew my cause. I wasn't seeing my buddy.

Rather than giving up my search in finding his number, I continued to look for it. As soon as I found it, I called him. He was glad to hear from me, and we set a time to see an evening matinee at a movie theater together. We had a blast. All through the summer, we called and talked to each other, and set times to visit one another. The summer was not as bad as I thought it would be.

Prior to that summer break, I had read a book by John Steinbeck called *Of Mice and Men*. It takes place during the Great Depression, and follows two friends who are bound by fate. Their names are George, an intelligent, caring, but rather cynical man, and Lennie, a strong but mentally challenged individual.

I don't want to spoil the story for those of you who haven't read it, but there's one part in the book that I remind myself of every day. Toward the end of it, the character George says, "A guy goes nuts if he ain't got nobody. Don't make no difference who the guy is, long's he's with you. I tell ya, I tell ya a guy gets too lonely an' he gets sick."

I learned from this comment and my summer experience that no person is meant to be alone. But it is ultimately up to each person to decide if they want to be isolated from everyone else or not.

I read in Proverbs 18:11 that, "One isolating himself will seek his own selfish longing; against all practical wisdom he will break forth." I may like my private time, perhaps more than most people that I know, but I don't make myself out to be a lonesome individual.

DIFFICULTIES MAKING FRIENDS

A lot of times I can tell if someone doesn't like me by the way they give me an odd or disgusted look. Usually, if someone gives me an unpleasant look, it's either because I'm doing something that person doesn't like, or maybe they just don't like my face. In my freshman and sophomore years, there was a kid I knew who had a lot of acne on his face. When he walked by, many girls would look the other way or cover their mouths with shock.

I felt sorry for the poor guy. Acne was not as big a problem for me as it was for some other teens that I knew. Still, I'm no chick magnet. One time when I was walking down the hallway to my locker, I spotted a rather attractive girl coming up the hallway, and said hello to her. She recoiled a bit, muttered a shy "Hi," and scurried away.

As a person with AS, I'm not good at interpreting body language, which makes it hard for me to make friends. I felt a bit abashed by this brief incident. I wondered for days if I had bothered this girl in any way. Had I done something wrong by speaking to her? Was she disgusted with me? Or did she like me and was too shy to talk to me directly?

Now that I am older, I now know I shouldn't get upset or worried about how a person sees me, nor should I take offense at nasty or odd looks from other people. It is not worth your time to contemplate whether a person likes you or not. It's all part of learning.

However, there are some exceptions—I do care if the important people in my life, my family and close friends, like me. I try not to bother with what strangers think of me. However, I am aware of how others view my physical appearance. During my days at school, many questions crossed my mind like, *how does my hair look? Do I have any visible pimples on my face? Do I smell bad?*

I try not to obsess over such self-awareness questions. I know that not everyone likes me, and it is not worth my time to try to please everyone. No one likes everybody.

In the past, I've had a habit of following too close to people when I walk behind them, whether it was in the school's hallway or at the cafeteria. One time, as I was waiting in the lunch line in grade school, I stood really close to the kid in front of me.

He turned around and said to me, "Why are you so close behind me?"

I looked at him, oblivious. "I am?"

"Yeah," he said with an elevated tone. "I can feel you breathing down my neck!"

"Oh, sorry," I said. I took several steps back from him and then I accidentally bumped into the kid behind me.

"Watch where you're stepping!" the kid behind me yelled.

"Sorry."

I don't know if I'm in a person's space unless the individual tells me. I try not to invade someone's space, I just don't know if I'm in it or not. I have grown out of this discommodity over the years.

Other times I have a tendency of talking endlessly about a specific topic. If someone mentions a movie, I become the chatterbox of the hour. Years ago, I went to a theater to see the film *Troy*. I was amazed by its splendid battle sequences and its epic storyline.

After my parents and I left the theater we went to get dinner. The whole time at the restaurant, I blabbered on about *Troy*, comparing and contrasting the movie with the myth, talking about all the trivia I have read about it on the Internet, and how spectacular it was on the big screen.

After probably about an hour of my consistent chatter on *Troy*, my mom got so tired of it that she said, "Jeff, can you shut up about *Troy*? Can we have a normal conversation, please?"

I could go on and on talking about a movie and not even know that I'm boring or even annoying the person I'm speaking to. I don't know if I am boring or irritating a person until the individual I'm talking to tells me that I am. The one thing I have learned about carrying on a conversation is that it can't be just one person talking the whole time. A conversation is carried on by two or more people, each taking turns to speak. If you ramble on, you won't hold a discourse very long.

I also have a habit of interrupting people while they speak. For instance, when my mom was on the phone, I would walk up to her and start talking about what I wanted to talk about. She would often put up her index finger. I would wait for a few minutes, and if she were still on the phone, I would start talking again. She would then wave me off or briefly put the phone aside and say, "Jeff, go away."

If she were talking to someone face to face, I would cut in, and start talking. It's rude to do things like these, but it's as if I just have an urge to talk. This was a habit of mine when I was six or seven, but sometimes I still do it—just not as frequently.

"You have to be patient with other people when they're talking," she would often tell me when I was little. "You can't just interrupt someone when they're in the middle of a sentence. Having a talk with someone takes as much listening as it does speaking. That's why you should take turns when you're chatting with someone. You have to hear both sides of the story."

Another bad habit I have is giving short answers when someone says "Hi" or "How ya doing?" I do this particularly in a crowded school hallway when my mind is so focused on getting to class on time that I forget everything else around me. With Asperger's Syndrome, I have a one-track mind. A person talking to me when I least expect it disrupts my routine. I don't like my routine to be interrupted.

Rather than saying, "Fine. How are you?" when someone says hello, I would say "Good," or "Is there something you need?" If that person did not respond right away, I would just walk away. People without AS perceive this as being rude. I try not to be rude; it's just how I respond.

When I did this in my junior high and early high school years, fewer and fewer people would say hello to me, and I constantly wondered why. I felt lonely and unaccepted by my peers. Then one day I came to realize that my blunt and brief replies were giving others the impression that I did not want to be bothered. I was just responding in my typical way.

Now if someone says, hello to me, I respond with something like "Hi, how are you?" If someone suddenly walks up and asks me a question, particularly when I'm trying to get to class on time, rather than cutting that person off I say something like, "I don't mean to be short with you, but I really need to get to class before the bell rings. If it's something quick, I can try to help."

HAVING ACQUAINTANCES

I always had difficulty differentiating between friends and acquaintances. Are they the same thing? An elder at the church I go to defined an acquaintance as "a person you know, may talk to, and get along with, but aren't close to. An acquaintance would be someone you wouldn't mind borrowing things from, but not to lend."

If every acquaintance I had were a friend, I would have a boatload of them. But I don't. I find that making acquaintances is easier than making close friends, because an acquaintanceship doesn't require you to know that person intimately, and is usually made up of casual conversations about school, after-class activities, and other things.

At the high school I transferred to for my junior and senior high school years, people seem to like me. I am mild-mannered, I don't get in trouble, and I'm almost an A- average student. I have made at least a dozen or so acquaintances during my two years there.

At the church I attend, there are a handful of different people that I talk to before and after the lesson. Members greet me with a smile or a "Hello." I respond with something like, "Good morning. Nice to see you again." "How have you been doing this week?" and I generally shake that person's hand. This always provides a good chance for me to start a conversation, as well as develop other acquaintances that might lead to friendships.

Acquaintances are a good thing to have. They can help you develop some social skills. Having acquaintances also makes me feel less lonely. It is better to have people to talk to, whether or not they're close pals.

WINNING FRIENDS

If you want to win friends, you must first learn to love yourself. I admit that it can be difficult to do at times. In the ninth grade, I once flunked a science test for which I had studied many hours during the days prior. I was absolutely furious with myself. When I came home from school, I went into my room and began ranting and raving, "How could you get an F on the test? You're now going to fail the class! You're a smart person, where was your brain?!"

I then reminded myself that my IEP allows me to retake tests if I get a poor grade on them. After I had vented all my anger, I tried to improve the rest of the day. Whether you are angry over flunking a test or going through some internal issue, on the whole, you must love yourself before pursuing the friendship of others.

Try to be yourself. I know it sounds corny, but it's dumber to pretend to be someone you are not. A lot of kids at my old high school love football. For years, when someone asked me about a sport, I acted like I was interested in it when, frankly, I don't care about sports. I pretended to be interested only so I could make friends, but then I felt worse, because I wasn't giving them my true opinion on the matter.

Instead of focusing on trying to enjoy something that I didn't really like in the first place, I decided to focus my attention on the positive aspects of myself rather than the negative. I have had a fascination with and interest in writing since as far back as the second grade. Throughout my junior high and high school years, I submitted my writing to be published in the school's literary magazine.

In the tenth grade, I got my fifteen minutes of fame when I had to write a poem on a topic of my choosing and present it to my Language Arts class. I picked the topic of love. When it came time to present my poem, I volunteered to be among the first to present. I approached the center of the class, took a few deep breaths, and read it as clearly as I could.

As I drew to a close, I received loud applause from the class. Several girls cheered and commented, "Jeff, that was a great poem!" "Jeff, you are so dead on with love!"

After class, a handful of girls surrounded me in the hallway and asked me for a copy of the poem I had written. As politely as I could, I told them I would get each of them a copy of the poem the following day. When I got home, I printed off several copies of the poem and gave them out the next day. I may not have earned any lady friends from this experience, but I did learn that people like individuals who are self-confident.

Try to find people who have interests that are similar to yours. If you like to write, see if there's an after-school curricular activity that involves writing. See if any interests you have apply to any after-school activities. I never participated in many extracurricular activities, but in the eighth grade, I was part of an after-school program that helped other students with homework.

There I met a girl who shared my interest in video games. After school, we would talk about the new video games that were out, and sometimes we would debate current controversial events.

Probably the majority of the friends I have made over my years at school were other loners or outcasts. In my seventh-grade study hall, I met a kid who many other students called a "freak" because he would sit alone at the back of the room and make weird noises during the class.

Kids would yell at him "Stop making that sound!" or "Shut your mouth, you dodo head!" I couldn't help but laugh at his strange sense of humor, which kept me awake in that first-bell study hall. I approached him one day and asked to sit down at his table. Ever since, he's been one of the people my age that I turn to for comic relief.

However, if you do enjoy your own company and would rather be on your own, there's nothing wrong with that. I'm a very introverted person. I still have friendships with a couple of kids at my high school, but most of my free time I spend alone.

Do not let anyone make you think otherwise. On a Friday in my eighth-bell study hall, my study hall teacher asked me, "So Jeff, what are you going to do this weekend?"

I shrugged.

"Are you going to the game?" she then asked.

"Game?"

"Yeah, the football game," she said.

"There's a football game here?" I asked.

"Yeah," she said. "Why, didn't you know?"

"No," I told her.

"If you're not going to the game, then what are you going to do to-night?" she asked.

"I don't know, play Halo, watch TV."

"Doesn't sound like much fun," she remarked.

"What?"

"Well, it sounds like a lonely night," she said. "Why don't you hang out with a couple of friends or something?"

Her words made me feel miserable and lonesome. I know she wasn't trying to make me feel bitter, but it's not good for someone, particularly an adult, to tell a teenager how to run his or her social life.

GROUPS OR INDIVIDUALS

Teenagers tend to travel in packs. Whenever I go to the mall and see a group of girls, I notice that only one or two of them are actually talking, while the others giggle, flick their hair, or nod their heads. I find it amazing that only one or two people (depending on the group's size) do all the speaking while the others just go with the group.

It's hard for me to participate in a group of four or more. When I'm in a group of people, for instance, during a school project, I can't keep up with the speed and frequency of the discourse. Usually those who do the most talking seem to ramble on about a certain topic. By the time I start to follow the chitchat, it often changes to a new subject.

In the background of the lead speakers, other members of the bunch would be having sidebar conversations. With two or more conversations going on simultaneously, I have a hard time deciding whom to listen to. I get confused, and feel that I'm not part of the group. When I'm lost, I feel unneeded. That's when I zone out.

If you have difficulty with group interactions, I suggest that you don't hang out in groups. If a friend asks you to join a group of his buddies after school or during the weekend and you don't feel up to it, do not say "yes" and go with him or her. Just say, "No thanks."

If he or she persists and asks why not, just respond truthfully. Say something like "I'm not up to it," or "I'm not interested." A true friend would understand your difficulty with group interactions. Do not make up an excuse.

There was a buddy of mine who asked me to go to a very late evening matinee with some of his pals. Rather than simply stating that I was tired and that I didn't want to stay up until two o'clock in the morning, I told him that I had a project to work on. I was so ashamed that I had lied to him. I felt like I was a bad friend. There's nothing worse than lying to a friend.

If you don't like being in groups of people, you can always meet with your friend and do an activity just with him, such as going to a movie or having him spend the afternoon at your house. I have found that doing a social activity with one friend at a specific location, such as at his house, is not such a strain, since I'm just with him.

Over one of my past summer breaks, I often went to a friend's house to play an online game with him that I did not own. Even though most of our time was consumed with gaming, we still got a chance to learn more about one another, and we had good times together. At his house, I did not feel overcrowded by several different individuals. I have always found one-on-one communication to be more enjoyable, and easier for me than group interactions.

However, there will be times you'll be in groups, whether it is with a friend who's with some of his pals at the theater, or for a group assignment in school. If you do want to join a friend and some of his pals, I would be cautious.

This has never been an issue for me, but some kids that I know at my high school have gotten into a world of trouble by hanging with their friends. Alcohol, drugs, and smoking are a growing problem among teenagers. I've seen kids after school lighting up cigarettes and throwing their butts on the ground. Make sure that the friends you do make are *not* involved in anything wrong, whether it is drugs, booze, smoking, or sex.

I always loathed group projects at school. It was my luck to always end up in the one group that goofed off, leaving me to do it all. If you happen to be put into a group that tends to goof off, ask permission from your teacher to be removed from that group. Or, if it is more comfortable for you, see if you can possibly work on the assignment independently. However, your teacher may very well pressure you to work in a group.

My tenth grade Language Arts teacher always told me, "Jeff, there will be times in your life that you'll have to work with other people. You can't always be a loner."

That's when you may have to compromise. Ask permission from

your teacher to be placed in a group that does their work. When put in a group for a school assignment, try to interact and be part of it. Work with the other students and do not withdraw or zone out. You can gain some acquaintanceships if you join in.

In my sophomore science class, I was put in a group with a couple of other students to do a PowerPoint project on the Earth. We had about a week to do the assignment, and all that time was spent in the computer lab. I did not know my group members well, so on the day we were given the assignment, I remained quiet and listened as they discussed what to do with the project.

After they chatted for a few moments, one of the group members asked me, "Jeff, what is your take on this?"

I said, "I think we should split up on our tasks. That way, we wouldn't have to worry about overwhelming ourselves with work. I am good with PowerPoint and researching."

My group found me invaluable. Throughout our days in the computer lab, they turned to me for guidance and assistance. Science was never my aptitude or intense area of interest, but I knew how to get assignments done efficiently and thoroughly. Not only did I become the leader of the group, but I also gained some acquaintances because of my work effort.

Note to Parents: Maturity and Helping with Social Issues

There are many different aspects of maturity to consider, including a person's physical, emotional, social, and intellectual development. I

165

physically matured like everyone else. I have grown body hair, all my baby teeth are gone, and I've gone though puberty. However, I did not speak until I was around the age of two or three. Instead of speaking "baby-talk" when I was about a year old, I spoke in full words and phrases.

When I was five years old, my kindergarten teacher gave me the assignment of drawing a picture of myself. She was probably thinking of a stick figure, but my brain had a different plan.

As soon as I got home from school, I got out a bunch of construction paper and drew and cut out a huge silhouette of myself. On the figure, I sketched all the various parts of the human body, including: the heart, brain, lungs, arteries, and veins. My kindergarten teacher did not know how to react to this.

Academically, I am ahead of many kids my age. Throughout my school years, I have maintained a GPA of almost 4.0. When I had to take the Ohio Graduation Test in my sophomore year, I scored in the top one percent in the subjects of history and math, and in the top ten percent in all the other subjects.

I am not trying to imply that all people with AS are intelligent and fully developed individuals. The kid I befriended who also has Asperger's Syndrome was not an A-average student.

When it comes to socializing, I don't understand body language or how to engage with other people. I also don't understand other people's emotions, which results in my not knowing how to react to them.

Presenting a project in front of the class was one of my biggest nightmares in school. Whenever I got the chance, I would bolt out the classroom door and flee to the nearest bathroom before it was my turn to present to the class. If a teacher told me that I had done badly on test, I would cry.

Now, my intention is not to explain what maturity is, or what is or isn't mature. My point is that each person matures at different levels. I am mature in some aspects but not in others. Each person with AS varies.

A part of my maturity is the result of being an only child. With no siblings around my age, I did not have anyone to teach me how to communicate with others my own age. From infancy to toddlerhood, I spent most of my time at home and at my aunt's house. I was often around adults, and this made it easy for me to bond and have friendships with most of my teachers. Many of my friends have been my past teachers in school.

In my early childhood years, though, my parents tried to make me associate with kids my age. When I was four, my parents took me to a daycare. They dropped me off in the morning and came back in the late afternoon to find that I had barricaded myself behind a line of blocks in a small corner. They thought I was just acting up. It wasn't until I was eleven that they learned about my AS condition.

The first time I attended daycare, I was surprised to see so many kids my age. The sight of them scared me. I felt more comfortable at home or at my aunt's house, because there I was mainly around adults and other relatives.

When my parents didn't have the time to watch over me, whether because of work or other matters, they would drop me off at the houses of friends who had kids my age. I would run around their house and hide anywhere I could. The kids would chase after me, thinking I was playing hide-and-seek, when I really just wanted to get away from them.

My parents took me to parks and a place called Children's World. I would always try to find a way to get away from other kids. It wasn't until I was six that I became best friends with the next-door neighbor's son. He and I would hang out on my backyard swing set, spend time at one another's house playing around, and we would even ride in the putt-putt car my dad bought.

When my parents tried to make me participate in the social world of kids, they were doing what they thought was right, but it only made me feel anxious and under pressure. It would be better to let your AS child find friends herself. If she doesn't try to make any friends, encourage her to do so, but don't make her feel that she has to have friends. Accept and respect your child's wishes if she doesn't seek out any friends in her early childhood years. I didn't get my first pal until I was six.

If she does want to give socializing a shot, that's great. But I suggest she start out with one or two friends and then grow from there. Having one close pal felt better to me rather than having a whole bunch of them. After I had befriended the next-door neighbor's son, I then branched off into making friends with the other neighborhood kids. By the time I was seven, I had well over a handful of pals that I hung out with.

In situations when your AS child is placed in a group for a school project, talk to the teacher and either make sure she is in a group of kids who do their work, or see if she can do the assignment independently.

As for emotional development, I can't give many suggestions. After I got past puberty, it was easier to handle my emotions. I got through the hardships of puberty with the help of medication, and the loving support of my parents. No matter what, you should be supportive of your AS child.

It is ultimately up to your AS child whether she is ready and willing to associate with others her own age. I have a couple of friends here and there, but I'm selective, and many of them are my fellow adult mentors.

Chapter 11

Dating and Relationships

I'm not that experienced in dating, nor am I good at maintaining relationships with people of the opposite sex. I have had only one girlfriend, and that was back in the second grade.

She had a cheerful attitude towards other people, and she had a good sense of humor. Our friendship started with us simply being acquaintances. We would talk to each other and sit together during lunch.

Then one day we decided to hang out with each other at recess and play tetherball. Since I wasn't good at sports or physical group activities, it was rather embarrassing. I would duck every time the ball came around the pole towards me. Unlike the other kids who would laugh at me and taunt me, she did not.

Instead, she encouraged me to play. She would say things like, "Jeff, you shouldn't duck when a ball comes at you. You should hit it."

Following our time together at recess, we started hanging out at my house after school. We would goof around, play on my backyard swing set or work on school assignments. Then one thing happened that I'll never forget.

As we were working on a project together in my house's office, she asked me, "Jeff, have you ever kissed a girl before?"

"Yeah, my mom," I replied.

"No," she said laughing. "I mean other than your mother."

I thought hard, not understanding where she was going with her strange question. After much contemplation, I said, "No."

"Do you want to?" she then asked.

I looked at her and then finally knew what she was implying.

I asked her, "You want me to kiss you, don't you?"

She nodded, blushing furiously.

"Uh, okay," I said with a shrug. I leaned forward, kissed her cheek, and quickly pulled away.

"No, I mean, on the lips," she then said.

It was my turn to change the color. Slowly and sheepishly, I leaned towards her again and kissed her quickly on the lips. As I pulled away from her, I thought, *I know I could do better than that to impress her.* I kissed her for a third time, and this time it was not just a peck on the lips. It was a romantic moment. But the only thing I got out of our special kiss was realizing how wet it was.

Since that moment, she and I became boyfriend and girlfriend. We had many great times together. My joy in spending time with her was as grand as a dream that had come true. I felt like a prince with a princess.

In addition to liking each other, we had many interests in common.

CHAPTER 11: Dating and Relationships

We both liked riding on roller coasters. We both enjoyed movies. She also enjoyed playing arcade and video games.

She and I even went on a trip during our second-grade spring break with my parents to Gatlinburg, Tennessee. However, there was something a little strange that happened when we went on that trip.

The hotel we stayed at had rooms big enough for only two beds. My parents split a bed, and my girlfriend and I split one. Every night when it was time for bed, my girlfriend would curl up real close to me, lean on me, and put her hand around my waist. At first I didn't take any of this seriously, but for the whole week we stayed at Gatlinburg, she did this.

On our last day there, I finally asked her before bed, "Why do you do that?"

"Do what?" she asked.

"Get real close and place your arm around me," I told her.

"Oh, I thought you liked it," she said. "Do you?"

"No, not really," I said.

She looked surprised by my response.

"Why?" she asked curiously.

I did not know how to explain to her that I was not comfortable being touched. I could not think of a reasonable answer. So I told her, "I just don't like to be touched, that's all."

"Is it because you're afraid of girl cooties?" she asked me. She then poked my belly with her finger.

"Stop it," I said.

"Stop what?" she asked, continuing to poke me.

"Stop touching me!" I said defensively.

"Well, sorry," she muttered.

She did not curl up next to me or touch me the rest of that night.

Back then, I didn't know about my AS so I could not explain to her about my sensitivity to touch. I loved to spend time with her, but I did not want to be physically involved with her. Besides, we were only in the second grade.

Despite the happiness and this odd action of hers, my girlfriend had a hidden, devastating secret. The following school year, I saw a guy talking to my girlfriend. I took no notice of their conversation at first, but I then I suddenly saw something that I never thought I would see my girlfriend do. She gave him a passionate kiss on the lips. I felt as though a spear had pierced my heart. *She was seeing someone else.*

The next day I encountered the guy in the cafeteria. A lot of bad words came from my mouth, and the other kid retaliated with equally foul language. It almost got to the point that I wanted to deck him, but the argument was broken up when another student overheard our quarrel and brought in a teacher to separate us.

As a result of this incident, I got a bad news note from school and a recommendation for a week's suspension. I did not get the suspension, but I was grounded for two weeks, and I was not permitted to watch any television during that time.

Shortly after this event, my girlfriend met up with me at recess and told me that she was moving away and that she was breaking up with me.

174

"Why?" I asked her. "Why are you dumping me? Did I do something wrong?"

"No it's just not working out," she said blandly.

"It's because of the other kid, isn't it?" I asked testily.

She sighed.

"Look, I like you, but he and I just get along better," she said.

Those words broke my heart. What did he have that I didn't? I did not ask that question, even though it was very tempting. I tried to take this anguish like a man by holding my emotions inside. I held them for the rest of the day at day school, but when I got home, I cried an ocean of tears.

THOSE FEELINGS

Years after our breakup I have been attracted to some girls, and I have made a few attempts at asking a couple of them out, but they always led to botched and rather embarrassing failures. I am no Prince Charming, but I definitely recognize the power that young ladies can hold over guys through their physical beauty.

When I see an attractive girl, I feel my emotions elevate as if I were smitten, and parts of my body become alive. Depending on how stunning the girl is or how close I am to her, my body comes to a halt and many old phrases come to mind like "butterflies in my stomach" and "legs turning to jelly."

The "butterflies in the stomach" describes the churning and discomfort I feel in my gut. The "legs turning to jelly" describes when my legs feel so numb and weak that I can't move or feel them. Other times my ears or my face gets hot, and occasionally I might feel shivers go down my back, which means my anxiety is jumping into play.

I find these kinds of feelings toward a girl unfamiliar; I am not used to such overwhelming physical reactions. I have asked my mom repeatedly if these feelings over a girl are normal.

"They are quite normal," she answered me several times. "You're a guy. It's a common thing for boys your age to like girls. It would be odd if you didn't feel this way over a girl."

I feel it is not right to have feelings of sexual arousal toward a girl. I find them to be a violation of my moral values. Whenever I have a sexual urge, I feel like another person is building inside of me, a monster that seeks carnal knowledge. It is very uncomfortable for me to write about this because even mentioning something like this creates physical distress in me.

With such odd feelings at the time of puberty and the teenage years, many guys are in competition with one another over girls by trying to win their sexuality. In the hallways at my high school, I would frequently see a mob of guys surround a couple of girls as if they were sharks seeking their prey, on which they want to feast.

As a person with Asperger's Syndrome, I don't join into the teen social world. I do my own thing. And unfortunately, doing my own thing makes many other teenagers at my high school perceive me as strange.

A lot of it is because of how I like to spend my free time. I would rather spend my time at home, watching a favorite movie or playing a game on a computer compared to hanging out with friends or going to a high school football game. I am different, and I am glad I am, but not everyone likes "different." This makes it hard for me to ask a girl out, much less talk to one whom I find attractive, or have a crush on.

There was one girl in my early high school years who I thought was flat-out gorgeous. I could not help but see her as a true beauty—in the league of actress Angelina Jolie. I would frequently daydream about her and me being together as boyfriend and girlfriend. But there was a voice in my head that held me back from asking her out.

"*Is she worth it?*" the voice would ask.

My heart said she was a perfect fit for me, but my mind was telling me something else. I know most romance films say such things as "follow your heart" and "love at first sight," but Proverbs 28:26 contradicts these movie clichés, saying that "He that is trusting in his own heart is stupid." Jeremiah 17:9 adds that, "The heart is more treacherous than anything else and is desperate."

I did not know what her personality was like. *Was she as beautiful inside as she was in her appearance?* I would often wonder. To help even more with my ambivalent feelings on the matter, I turned back to reading the *Questions Young People Ask* book. Under the section of dating, it brought up several questions:

- Has the person you like shown any interest in you at all?
- Is there a real reason to believe that things will change in the future of him or her liking you?

177

- Or are you simply reading romantic interest into innocent words and actions on his or her part?[1]

This girl would at times twirl her hair, smile and say "Hi" to me. I wasn't sure whether she was smiling at me because she liked me or just out of politeness. I always hoped it was out of affection.

Again, as an individual with Asperger's Syndrome, it is hard for me to understand body language. My feelings for this girl clouded my judgment for a long time. There were days I felt that I could not concentrate in class or even sleep at night.

Then one day, I saw her at a grocery store with another guy who looked to be in his late teens or early twenties. I knew it could not be her dad because he looked too young. Nor could it be her brother because of the way I saw how he had his hand wrapped around her waist. *Another guy already had taken her.* This realization devastated me.

After seeing this, I would often wish, and even pray, that she would break up with her boyfriend and come to me instead. It may have been wishful thinking on my part, but deep down, I knew that wishing for such a thing was selfish and wrong. Such thinking would have also fed my fantasy of her.

I knew she was not the girl for me because she was already dating someone else, and there was no point hoping or waiting for something that wasn't going to happen.

To help myself get over this crush, I kept reading my copy of the *Questions Young People Ask* book. In one of the chapters I read under the section of Dating, a writer named Kathy McCoy stated that "immature love can come and go in a moment. ... The focus is on you and you're simply in love with the idea of being in love."[2]

Immature love is not *true love*. Living a fantasy about someone, whether it is a pop star, a teacher, or even someone your age, is not worth your time. Besides, most teen boyfriend and girlfriend relationships don't usually last after high school, because students go their separate ways to different colleges, universities, or jobs. Some students may never see each other again.

My dad always went to his high school reunions, and at each one he went to he told me that he never saw the friends he had hung out with in high school. "People get their new and separate lives after school," he told me after the last reunion he went to. "Some may never even see each other again. Things change. People change."

Thus, most teenage relationships are doomed. My mom told me that, of the kids who had dated each other back when she was in high school, only one couple has remained together since then. Most teen relationships are based on physical attraction.

I read further in *Questions Young People Ask* book in which a Dr. Charles Zastrow states that, "Infatuation occurs when a person idealizes the person he or she is ... with as being a perfect lover; that it concludes the other person has all the characteristics desired."[3]

It is important to consider this information before starting to date someone. Remaining ignorant about relationships and sex can have life-long repercussions. For example, many teens I know who were sexually active in high school ended up getting pregnant or an STD. And in many of those cases, their actions were based more on physical attraction than mutual respect; they were acting upon their bodily urges rather than taking it slow and being safe.

But there's much more to relationships than just sex. You'll need to consider social and emotional aspects as well. You can't predict whether someone else will be open to or ready for a relationship, but you can take steps to make sure that *you* are ready before you move forward. When I want to date someone, I ask myself several questions:

- Am I ready to date?
- Am I prepared to open myself up to another person I don't know or that I don't know very well?
- Will another person understand and accept my AS condition?

These are hard questions to ask myself. I am well aware that not everyone understands or even knows about Asperger's Syndrome. Some people may not even care to understand it. This makes it all the more difficult for me to find someone my age who could comprehend my AS, much less go out with me.

I don't want to influence your opinion or view on dating, but I feel that dating isn't worth it until I am an adult and ready for a fully committed relationship. Dating is not for everyone in the teenage years, for it requires a lot of social interaction. As I've illustrated many times earlier in this book, as a person with AS, socializing is not my specialty.

CHAPTER 11: Dating and Relationships

If you do want to date, then give it a shot. But you must overcome your shyness and the fear of rejection. You must also be willing to accept criticism from other kids in school. Rumors of "who likes whom" and "who's dating whom" spread quickly as a forest fire in high school.

Before you decide to date someone you like, I suggest you become her friend first. Start as acquaintances and see if it grows. If it grows, you could become more than acquaintances, and possibly develop a close friendship.

There was a girl I knew back in the eighth grade who was very nice, easy to get along with, and had a very cheerful attitude towards others. By the way she smiled at me, I sensed that she liked me, and I had a little bit of a crush on her.

Instead of running up to her and asking her out, I started making small talk with her so I could get to know her a little better. I asked her questions like: "How's the school year going for you?" or "Anything exciting going on over the weekend for you?"

We later started studying together for Language Arts class and visited one another at lunch. We also exchanged phone numbers. I did not feel pressured into dating her nor did she seem to feel pressured by me.

After knowing her for a few months, I decided to make a move. I thought the best way to win her heart was by buying her a gift. My mom told me that, "The best time of year to give a gift to a girl is on Valentine's Day."

I went to a Hallmark store and bought her a pair of earrings for thirty dollars. With all my courage on that Valentine's Day, I approached her in the hallway and handed the earrings to her. When she opened the box, she immediately looked up at me as if Christmas had come early.

She threw her arms around me. At first I did not know how to react. I was so surprised and shocked that I stood still as her arms wrapped around me. I never would have hugged anyone, unless it was out of affection. I slowly placed my arms around her. We held each other for a full, eternal moment.

"You really made my day," she told me after she let go of me. From this action, I thought she liked me. So, I decided to press forward and to see if our romance would grow.

After I had given her the earrings, I started writing letters to her about how much I was touched by her hug and that I had feelings for her. After I sent her three letters over a month's time, she did not approach me in the hallways anymore or in the Language Arts class we were in together. When I started to talk to her, she would ignore me and keep walking.

For months, I tried to regain her favor with more written letters, phone calls, and encounters in the hallway. She seemed to do whatever she could to avoid me. One time I was walking down a hallway alone when she suddenly came around the corner at the end of it. As soon as she saw me, she stopped, quickly turned around, and ran back around the corner.

Another time, I approached her at her locker and asked, "Is something wrong? Why won't you talk to me?"

She got very angry and said, "Jeff, I've got to get to band! I can't be late to class."

CHAPTER 11: Dating and Relationships

It became more than obvious that she did not share the same affection for me as I did for her. It came to the point that her parents called me and told me to "back off." It was hard for me to let go: I couldn't take no for an answer, but that was the only thing I could do. I gave up on her, with a broken heart.

If you want to risk trying to win a girl's heart, you can give it a try. Give her a gift only when you feel up to it. A card would be a nice gift, but don't buy her a necklace that costs a couple hundred dollars, or a bouquet of roses. That's a bit over the top. The last thing you want to do is make a fool of yourself, or scare her away.

Giving someone you don't know well an expensive gift can overwhelm that person, and she might get the idea that you are obsessed with her. My letters, phone calls, and encounters in the hallways may have given the girl I liked the impression that I was stalking her. That was not my intent; however, such actions can be easily misunderstood. Be careful and don't obsess over someone you have a crush on.

Back in my early teenage years, I had issues with self-esteem and wanted to be accepted at school. I felt that if this girl were my girlfriend, then that would happen. I feel this is a normal way of thinking for most teenagers.

If you have this sort of issue, I suggest you talk to someone about it. I know what it is like to not want to live without a companion. It is a painful thing to go through. I always talked to my parents and therapist about the situation with this girl. The more I talked about it, the less of a burden it became. It has been four years since it happened, and I rarely think about her any more.

If you do decide to give a gift to someone and you do ask her out, and she declines, or much worse, laughs at you, don't take offense. I know it may feel insulting, but on the bright side, you know that the person you like isn't interested in you, so you can move on and find someone else.

TIPS TO ENHANCE YOUR CHANCES OF DATING

In the past I wouldn't clean my hair or brush my teeth. With Asperger's Syndrome, I am not overly concerned with how others see me. But this habit of mine changed when people began telling me how horrible my breath smelled, and a lot of times, I would find bits of dandruff on my clothes. In addition, my head would itch like crazy.

When I scratched my head to get rid of the itchiness, more dandruff would come out of my hair, as if I was making snowflakes. To avoid such problems, always take care of your hygiene. Bathe, clean your hair, brush your teeth at least twice a day, and use deodorant.

I'm not the best with this, but you may want to experiment with your looks. Wear a new style of clothing or get a new haircut. With a new look, you could attract attention. But I wouldn't go overboard with your appearance.

Many of the girls at my high school spend their free time at the tanning salons. There was a girl I knew in the tenth grade who loved to go to tanning salons so much that she went three times a week. One day, she came to school with her skin so badly burned that she looked like a lobster.

Later on, I read in an article that said too much sunlight and tanning can various skin cancers.[4] You don't have to look like the next Tom Cruise or Jessica Alba to get people's attention.

A couple of years ago, I asked a friend of mine who was very outgoing on how he got girls to like him so much. He laughed and said, "As corny as it sounds, just be yourself. It's not worth being something that you're not. Girls like guys who are true and honest."

I've always been myself, but I don't open myself up to other people a whole lot. To a degree, I still don't. I like my privacy. If a person you like asks you a question, don't clam up; be open to discussion.

There was a girl in my tenth-grade Language Arts class who asked me if I was at a certain restaurant a day prior. I froze when she spoke to me; I was uncertain how to answer her question. I did not particularly have a crush on her, but I was shocked. *A girl was speaking directly to me? How should I reply?* I wondered.

"I work there," she then said.

"Huh?"

"At LaRosa's," she said. "I work there part-time."

"Oh, I wouldn't know," I responded.

"You don't have to be a moron about it. I'm just asking you a question," she said indignantly.

I had unintentionally cut her off. I know it can be difficult to talk to someone, and it is even more challenging to try not to be blunt or insolent with answers. Never cut a person off or interrupt them when they are talking to you. If you do, they will think you're stuck up. People appreciate politeness. It may not feel rude to you, but other people may perceive it as such.

Also remember that not everyone will approach you. I always dreamed that my relationship with any girl that I liked would begin when she ran up to me and said that she liked me. Well, that most likely won't happen. Most boyfriend and girlfriend relationships that I have heard about start when the guy takes the initiative by asking the girl out; however, I've also seen girls ask guys out.

Many relationships start with a simple incident: one person asking another person a question about a geometry test, for example. If there's a guy or girl you like, it is mainly up to you to ask him or her out. This is one of the most impossible things for me to do. There's not a whole lot of advice I can give you on how to ask someone out or even what it is like to be on a date. I could give you a list of "do's and don'ts" on asking a person out and on a first date, but it would be unfair for me to give you a bunch of tips that I have never tried out myself.

Your parents are the best people to turn to on the matter of dating and how to ask a person out. They were young once too, and they've had experience dating. Their tips would be far more beneficial than mine.

A TIP FOR YOU LADIES

For you female AS readers, when you do go on a date or are dating someone, keep your wits about you. Follow your mind rather than your heart. Intimate desires are common among teenagers, but don't let them get the best of you and never let a guy force you to do something that you don't want to do, whether it involves touching personal body parts, or even sex. Always speak up.

A person may date someone just because of sexual or physical attraction, but that rarely develops into a relationship. Having relationships with the opposite sex involves social interactions, sharing activities with a person who has interests similar to yours—not just dating a person because of their good looks. However, one person's view of dating may be totally different from another's.

Dating can also be a simple time when a boy and girl do some sort of casual activity together, like seeing a movie at a theater—just having a good time. On the other hand, it could be a serious time, when two people want to learn about each other, and then they might want to meet for dinner at a fancy restaurant. It all comes down to two people of the opposite gender seeing each other under a variety of circumstances.

Dating is a very serious matter. It is a way to meet someone with whom you can be friends, or develop a more serious relationship. Whatever way you look at dating, I hope you appreciate spending time with a person you like and are interested in.

Chapter 12

Obsessions and Creativity

In early childhood years, kids can be obsessed with or have a special interest in things they possess: toy cars, a stuffed animal, K'NEX™, a soccer ball, or many other things. From the ages of one to twelve years old, I clung mostly to my teddy bear, "Bee." Everywhere I went, I had to have him with me. The only time I did not have him with me was at school. At school, I yearned to go home to see and hug my teddy bear.

Another thing I liked to do when I was little was to collect things. Around the ages of six to nine, I collected miniature crystals from the amusement park Kings Island. I also liked to collect colored crayons, pencils, matchbox cars, and Beanie Babies™.

Eventually though, I grew out of my fixation on collecting things and my teddy bear Bee. But there's one thing I have never been able to get enough of since the age of five, and that is movies. Since I saw the films *Star Wars*, *Raiders of the Lost Ark*, and *E.T.*, I cannot stop talking about them.

I don't enjoy movies just for their entertainment value. I mainly enjoy them because I know the amount of detail and work it takes to make them. I like to go in-depth about how they are made, who's in what position, whether it is the director, the music composer, the actors, or even the video and audio editors.

Knowing all the different talents it takes to make a film really fascinates me. As an individual with Asperger's Syndrome, I can't let go of my intense, special interest in movies. I've read several articles that say that a common characteristic of persons with AS is having narrow interests or fixations on certain things or topics.

What makes such a fixation difficult is that special interests can dominate a person with a condition like AS. For years, it has been challenging for me not to talk about movies, and it is usually about the three movies listed above. It's like an impulse I have. I need to say something about them, or go berserk.

And what's strange about it is that, when I'm not thinking about them, it somehow pops out of my mouth when I have nothing else to say. It is as if the topic of movies has bypassed my mind and infiltrated my mouth—like a surprise attack from a special ops team. A lot of this happens to me when I'm at dinner with my parents. When I have nothing else to talk about, I immediately start to talk about movies.

As for collecting things, I mainly collect movie soundtracks. The movie soundtracks I collect, though, have different styles, and are usually composed by one of three composers: John Williams, Hans Zimmer, and James Horner.

CHAPTER 12: Obsessions and Creativity

CONTROLLING AN OBSESSION

It is fine to have a special interest in something, but not when it controls your mind. Having an obsession that dominates your conversations with people can make you a social outcast.

I've learned that people don't want to hear me talk about my fixations over and over again. It irritates them. It bores people, and it can label me as a "weirdo."

To illustrate this, I knew a girl in my junior high school digital-design class who had a very cordial attitude to others. But whenever I or someone else would get into a discussion with her, she would talk only about what she wanted to talk about. She was a very talented artist and worked with animation programs like Photoshop and Flash, but she talked only about her artwork. "How does this look?" "What do you think of this?" or, "I got this idea from this." Whenever she would approach someone, that person would often roll his or her eyes or mutter something like, "Uh-oh, here she comes."

She was a nice individual but she alienated herself from other people by talking only about her artwork. Every talk you have that is about the same thing is like watching the same movie over and over again. You get tired of hearing about and seeing it after a while.

I have to admit, though, that when I was little, I could watch the same film over and over again and not be bored. When I was five, I watched the movie *Dumbo* three times in a row without getting bored. Most people I know couldn't do that.

It is ultimately up to you to control your obsession or special interest. Pills and other people cannot help with this. But there are ways I have found that can control my obsessions. It comes down to creativity.

You can put your obsession into good use by being creative with it. What I've done with my intense interest in movies is to join a program at a vocational school that is about moviemaking, called digital design.

At the high school I transferred to, half my day is spent on video and audio editing, working a camera, designing animated characters and many other things, while the other half of my day is spent in four academic classes. Since I've been involved in a moviemaking program at school, I feel less of an oddball, because I am around other individuals my age who, like me, are interested in films.

On my own, I have made more than a handful of movies so far in my digital design class. None of them are feature-length films, but I have some experience in what it takes to make a movie.

The other thing I have done with my special interest in movies was to join a worldwide organization called *imdb*. At this website, I rate and write reviews for movies. After four years, I have rated more than eight hundred movies, and written over a hundred film reviews.

I can't tell you how you can be creative with any obsession or special interest you have. I suggest you try to find ways with any fixation or special interest you have by getting involved with others. For instance, if you like to write, see if there's a creative writing class, or a place for you on the school newspaper. Remember, some individuals with AS have used their special interests and obsessions to make great things.

Chapter 13

To Sum Up

When they hear the words "Asperger's Syndrome" or even "autism," most people probably think of the film *Rain Man*, which features a cool middle-aged guy who's an absolute genius with numbers. But this kind of individual, portrayed wonderfully by actor Dustin Hoffman, was an "autistic savant."[1]

In my opinion, this gives the general public the idea that all people on the autistic spectrum, including those with AS, have some sort of supernatural ability, which is far from the truth. Savantism is a very rare condition on the autistic spectrum. According to an article I read titled "Autistic Savant," it states that, "... the estimated prevalence of savant abilities in autism is 10%."[2]

Even more aggravating, people degrade us for being different. People in this world can be bad, unfair, or even misled. But there are also good people. My dad always reminds me that there is more good than bad in the world, and that the good always outweighs it.

Now I'm not denying that there'll be times that'll seem hopeless.

It's just part of the ups and downs of life. A lot depends on what you focus on. If you dwell on the bad, you'll only feel bad. If you persevere with the good, you'll feel better. Focus on the good traits you have, rather than your disadvantages. I'm ignorant about social activities, but I have a high intellectual level. With your advantages, you can strive for excellence.

You have much to look forward to.

Since this is the end of the book, I would like to say that I hope it has come in handy for those of you with Asperger's Syndrome, and for parents who have children with Asperger's. Those of you with AS may still wonder, after reading this book, why you have Asperger's Syndrome. The truth is, no one knows. Scientists all over the world are still trying to figure that out. But what we do know is that people with Asperger's can lead very successful and fulfilling lives. So no matter how challenging things get from day to day, always remember that you are not alone. There are others out there like you, and like me, who are facing similar challenges, and who are succeeding more and more each day. There is much for you, AS readers and parents, to look forward to in life.

Notes

CHAPTER I

1. "Asperger Disorder." *American Academy of Child and Adolescent Psychiatry*. 69 (1999): 7-8. Web. 18 June 2010. http://www. aacap.org/cs/root/facts_for_families/aspergers_disorder.

2. "Asperger's Syndrome." *Syncrat*. Syncrat. 2010. Web. 18 June 2010. http://www.syncrat.com/articles/aspergers.

3. Newport, Jerry. *Your Life Is Not a Label*. Texas: Future Horizons Inc.

4. "Hans_Asperger." 2010. *Reference.com*. Dictionary.com, LLC. 2010. Web. 18 June 2010. http://www.reference.com/browse/ wiki/Hans_Asperger.

5. See note 4, above.

6. See note 4, above.

7. See note 4, above.

8. See note 4, above.

9. See note 4, above.

10. See note 4, above.

11. "Results of Autism Study Could Help Researchers with Early Detection and Measuring Severity of Condition." *Yale University of Public Affairs*. Yale. 10 Oct. 2002. Web. 18 June 2010. http://opa.yale.edu/news/article.aspx?id=3123.

12. See note 11, above.

13. "What is the difference between autism and Asperger's Syndrome?" *Autisam SA*. Autism Association of South Australia Inc., trading as Autism SA. 2005. Web. 18 June 2010. http://www.autismsa.org.au/html/disorders/difference.html.

14. See note 13, above.

15. Attwood, Tony. "Is There a Difference Between Asperger's Syndrome and High Functioning Autism?" Sacramento Asperger Syndrome Information and Support. Sacramentooasis.com. 2010. Web. 18 June 2010. http://www.sacramentoasis.com/docs/8-22-03/as_&_hfa.pdf.

16. See note 1, above.

17. See note 1, above.

CHAPTER 3

1. "The Benefits of Light Therapy Lamps." Light Therapy Lamps. http://www.therapylamp.com.

2. MayoClinic. "Light Therapy." *MayoClinic.com*. Mayo Foundation for Medical Education and Research. 2010. Web. 18 June 2010. http://www.mayoclinic.com/health/light-therapy/my00195.

CHAPTER 4

1. Frances, Nelle. "Asperger's Syndrome and Unequal Reaction to Pain." *Lazarum.com*. Lazarum.com. 2010. Web. 18 June

2010. http://www.lazarum.com/2/en/articles/articles_view. php?idarticulo=5.

CHAPTER 5

1. "Fine motor skills." 2010. *Reference.com.* Dictionary.com, LLC. 2010. Web. 18 June 2010. http://www.reference.com/browse/ finc+motor+skills?o=100074.
2. Kiefaber, Matt. "Video Games." *PsyberSite.* PsyberSite, Miami University. 25 Jan 2010. Web. 18 June 2010. http://www.units. muohio.edu/psybersite/cyberspace/onlinegames/video.shtml.
3. See note 2, above.
4. See note 2, above.
5. Kitto, Julie, et al. "Gross Motor Skills." *Motor Development.* Flinders University. 6 Feb 2009. Web. 18 June 2010. http:// ehlt.flinders.edu.au/education/DLiT/2000/FINAL/gross-motors.htm.

CHAPTER 6

1. Mayo Clinic. "Stress symptoms: Effects on your body, feelings, and behavior." *MayoClinic.com.* Mayo Foundation for Medical Education and Research. 2010. Web. 18 June 2010. http:// www.mayoclinic.com/health/stress-symptoms/sr00008_d.
2. See note 1, above.
3. "Depression in Children and Teens-Topic Oveview." *WebMD.* WebMD, LLC. 2010. Web. 18 June 2010. http://

www.webmd.com/depression/tc/depression-in-childhood
-and-adolescence-topic-overview.

4. See note 3, above.

5. *Questions Young People Ask: Answers That Work*. New York:
   Watchtower Bible and Trace Society of New York, Inc.

CHAPTER 9

1. Wohlfell, Carol. "What makes a child become a bully." Helium.
   Helium, Inc. 2010. Web. 18 June 2010. http://www.helium.
   com/items/273175-what-makes-a-child-become-a-bully.

CHAPTER 10

1. See note 5, under Chapter 6.

CHAPTER 11

1. See note 5, under Chapter 6.

2. See note 5, under Chapter 6.

3. See note 5, under Chapter 6.

4. "What Should I Know Before Using a Tanning Bed?" *All Tanning Beds*. All Tanning Beds. 2008. Web. 18 June 2010.

5. http://www.all-tanning-beds.com/tanning-faq/what-should-i-
   know-before-using-a-tanning-bed.html.

CHAPTER 13

1. Edelson, Stephen. "Autistic Savants." *Autism Research Institute*. Autism Research Institute. 2010. Web. 18 June 2010. http://www.autism.com/fam_autistic_savants.asp.

2. See note 1, above.

Index

K

Karate (martial arts), 134, 149

Kissing, 172

L

Labels, 10

Lamp therapy, 37

Language. *See also* communication
   age of development, 166
   AS versus autism, 7
   learning, 113–126

Law enforcement, 137–138

Learning, 21

Licenses, automobile, 102–104

Limitations, 3

Listening, 126, 157

Loneliness. *See also* solitude
   AS and, 2, 7, 151, 194
   acquaintances and, 159
   adults and, 162
   basics, 152–153
   bluntness and, 157
   friendships and, 151–152
   self-control and, 51

Love, 179. *See also* dating and
   girlfriends

M

Machines, 44, 45

Mad hatters, 114–115

Males, AS and, xi

Malls, 44

MapQuest, 107–108

Martial arts, 134, 149

Maturity, 167

McCoy, Kathy, 179

Medication
   basics, 6, 8–9
   depression and, 81, 82–83
   Seasonal Depression and, 36, 37
   sleep and, 75

Meltdowns, 67–69, 73, 74, 101

Memory, x, 59

Mental health days, 39

Metaphors, 114

Of Mice and Men (Steinbeck), 153

Middle school, 21

Mindfulness, 62–63. *See also* focus
   (attention, concentration)

Misinterpretations, 119–120, 123–125

Mistakes, 15

Moods, 35–36, 121. *See also specific
   moods*

Motor skills, 55–65

Movies. *See also* theaters; *specific
   movies*

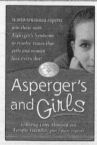

Positive Stories, Practical Strategies, Proactive Solutions!

Since 1999,
providing **real life**
information for meeting
the **real life** challenges
of ASD.

"If only I knew about your magazine 5 years ago, my child's life would have turned out significantly different."

— *Carol, Parent*

2009 Gold Winner

Gold Winner
three years in a row!
2007 - 2009

Join our mailing list for free publications, subscription discounts, and special offers! www.AutismDigest.com